Birth
Control
for
Christians

Birth
Control
for
Christians

Making
Wise Choices

JENELL WILLIAMS PARIS

Baker Books
A Division of Baker Book House Co
Grand Rapids, Michigan 49516

Published by Baker Books
a division of Baker Book House Company
P.O. Box 6287, Grand Rapids, MI 49516-6287
www.bakerbooks.com

Printed in the United States of America

Library of Congress Cataloging-in-Publication Data
Paris, Jenell Williams.
  Birth control for Christians : making wise choices / Jenell Williams Paris.
       p.   cm.
  Includes bibliographical references.
  ISBN 0-8010-6437-6 (pbk.)
    1. Contraception—Religious aspects—Christianity. 2. Contraception—Popular
  works. 3. Birth control—Moral and ethical aspects. I. Title.
  RG136.2 .P365 2003
  613.9′4—dc2   2003000133

This book has been written and reviewed by experts, but it does not claim to take the place of qualified medical advice or treatment. This book is designed to be informational, not instructional. Precise instructions regarding method or use must be obtained from qualified instructors. Therefore, the author, publisher, editors, and reviewers cannot be responsible for any error, omission, or dated material. Please contact your doctor or other fertility expert regarding medical matters. The author and publisher assume no responsibility for any outcome of the use of these methods in a program of self-care or under medical supervision.

Scripture is taken from the New Revised Standard Version of the Bible, copyright 1989 by the Division of Christian Education of the National Council of the Churches of Christ in the USA. Used by permission.

For James

Contents

Acknowledgments

I wrote this book as a gift to my fellow believers, yet I too have been blessed by all I have received along the way. The spirit of this book has been most influenced by the marriage I share with James and by the friends and family who help us stay in love.

Bethel College funded my participation at the Houghton Institute for Integrative Studies, a beautiful summer seminar where my writing began. At the Houghton Institute, Glenn Tinder and the seminar participants provided support and critique in the early stages of writing. Bethel also provided funds for illustration and a Faculty Development Grant for research materials. Even more importantly, Bethel provided a creative, peaceful, and well-lit environment for thinking and expressing good things.

Many individuals contributed time, energy, and love to this project. Close reading and helpful critique came from Jay Barnes, Ben Braff, Robin Carlson, Karen Drake, Katie and Ben Holmgren, RaeAnne LaBelle, Neil Lettinga, Matt Palmer, and Jennifer Scott. Student researchers included Kara Rafferty and Robyn Minahan, and essential student support came from Ann Barrett, Seng Vang, Lindsay Norman, and Natalie Olsen. My social science colleagues James Hurd, Harley Schreck, and Samuel Zalanga provided encouragement along the way. Medical review came from Marcos

Arevalo, Janice Schreck, Markus Steiner, and Melissa Wanner. Wendy Van Dilla from the Ovulation Method Teacher's Association and Anne Lanctot from the Archdiocese of Washington, D.C., first taught me about fertility and natural approaches to birth control. Students in my fertility awareness course (Fertility Awareness–Twin Cities) have asked good questions and shared their stories. Ruby, Mattie, and Opal Paris entertained me and listened patiently throughout this project. My teachers and colleagues at the American Studies Program of the Council for Christian Colleges and Universities, especially Steve Garber, Jerry Herbert, and Joan Orgon-Coolidge, taught me so well that when I write about *shalom*, I think the ideas are my own. Margot Eyring helped me learn about making wise choices and valuing health in a holistic way.

Introduction

When I was single, I sometimes thought about the man I might marry, the wedding I might plan, the house we might live in, and the children we might enjoy. I didn't, however, think much about condoms, pills, and diaphragms, or the ethics surrounding these complex technologies. As a single Christian, talking about contraception seemed dangerous because it might imply that I was having sex, planning to have sex, or thinking about planning to have sex. Sex was taboo in word and deed, and this hushed climate contributed to my naiveté about birth control.

In a prewedding search for information about birth control, I found two rich sources of guidance, secular sexual health guides and Catholic moral teachings. They were helpful, but each had significant limitations. I learned anatomy and the basics of contraception from *Our Bodies, Ourselves,* a popular secular guide to women's health. In a discussion of contraceptive choices, however, the authors state that "safe, affordable" abortion is an essential part of full reproductive freedom. In their view, we women "have a right to control our own bodies and . . . we must organize to secure that right in the face of attacks by church, state, and the organized right wing."[1] This secular philosophy encourages women to create their own morals, to make nearly any sexual choice, and to control fertility through any type of contraception or abortion. While I needed the medical information in this book, I

11

knew the information was presented within a framework that was at odds with my Christian worldview. Because most of the information was new to me, however, I couldn't easily sort the good information from the authors' biases. I learned a lot about sex and birth control, but I wanted to do more than avoid pregnancy. I wanted to do the right thing.

My Catholic housemate encouraged me to look into natural family planning (NFP). The Catholic views presented to me at natural family planning courses were more helpful in terms of morality. My instructor emphasized the sacredness of life and the holiness of marriage and sex, reinforcing my belief that all choices and the motives behind them have moral dimensions. In *Humanae Vitae* (Of Human Life), a papal encyclical issued in 1968, Pope Paul VI explained the Catholic Church's position on the regulation of birth: "The problem of birth, like every other problem regarding human life, is to be considered . . . in the light of an integral vision of man and of his vocation, not only his natural and earthly, but also his supernatural and eternal vocation." So far so good, in my mind. The pope continued, stating that by God's design and by church tradition, "each and every marriage act must remain open to the transmission of life."[2] According to traditional Catholic teaching, contraception and sterilization are sinful because they interrupt God's full and natural purposes of conjugal love. My Protestant faith tradition, however, teaches that people may use birth control to plan their families wisely and that marriages grow strong when a young couple can spend their first few years focusing on the maturity of their relationship. While I respected the moral reflections of the pope and of my Catholic instructor, I did not come to agree with their understanding of conjugal love and contraception.

By reading both Catholic and secular sources, my fiancé and I pieced together our own philosophy and practice of fertility control. We appreciated the self-knowledge and Christian perspective of NFP but did not believe mandated periods of abstinence were a necessary part of Christian sexuality. We discovered the fertility awareness method (FAM), which allowed us to chart and interpret my cycle and encouraged barrier methods (e.g., condoms and diaphragms) or abstinence during fertile times to avoid pregnancy. The secular sexual health books were helpful because from them we learned about anatomy, sexuality, and birth control options in broad scope. Catholic NFP courses helped us reason within a Christian framework as we strove to consider the moral implications of each decision.

I still wonder why, on the issue of contraception, secular feminists and Roman Catholics are the most outspoken and thoughtful guides. These movements have obvious interests in marriage, sexuality, and reproduction, but so do procontraception Christians. Where are their voices? While both Catholic and secular sources are helpful, each has limitations. The Catholic readings stopped at the first question — the acceptability of contraception — and the secular readings worked from moral premises different from my own.

In the years since my engagement and marriage, I have continued to learn about birth control and have found rich conversation about sexuality, life changes, and family planning with singles, engaged couples, and married couples in my college courses, church, and fertility awareness courses. These conversations, as well as my personal experience, provided inspiration for this book. I hope to guide you, the reader, to important questions associated with contraceptive choices. Because couples live with the consequences of their choices, it is essential that they reflect upon and confidently make their own decisions rather than simply accept what parents, friends, or medical professionals advise. James (my husband) and I concluded, for example, that the fertility awareness method (see chapter 5) provided us with the responsibility, self-knowledge, and contraceptive effectiveness we wanted. This method avoided the ethical and medical complexities of hormonal methods (see part 4) but didn't require us always to use a condom or diaphragm. I know readers will reach different conclusions that make sense within their life circumstances and their understanding of Christianity. So, rather than pushing my own conclusions, I will walk with you through this complex terrain, sharing my insights and asking, where appropriate, what I hope will be helpful questions.

As for my background, most significantly I am a Christian woman who makes personal fertility management decisions. I share my story because contraceptive decisions are part of our life stories, with surrounding hopes, fears, and expectations that are unique to each couple. In addition, I am a fertility awareness instructor, certified with the Ovulation Method Teacher's Association. I have taught fertility awareness to women and couples since 1999 and have learned much by listening to their questions and stories. I am also a professor of anthropology at a Baptist liberal arts college, and I research and teach about sex and gender. For this book, Robyn Minahan and I conducted a small qualitative study about how Christians make birth control choices.[3] I used insights from this study, medical research, and my fertility awareness teaching experience to develop the information and questions in this book. When I refer to quotes and stories from people's lives, I use a pseudonym and approximate age to protect anonymity.

It's difficult to sort through contraception within a Christian perspective for several reasons. Sex and contraception are freely discussed in the United States and other contemporary cultures but often in a way that is devoid of biblical ethics. For example, Planned Parenthood's latest birth control book, *All about Birth Control: The Complete Guide,* intends "to guide you in your most private choices and to provide you with information about the public and political conflicts that challenge your right to privacy and your right to choose."[4] In our society birth control is radically individualized and privatized, excluding even male sexual partners from a woman's decisions. It's often difficult and sometimes impossible to obtain new information and filter it ethically at the same time. It's also difficult to learn about medical processes and technologies because they are so complex and because medical language is impossible for nonexperts to understand.[5]

This book provides current medical information about contraception and encourages dialogue, all within a Christian perspective. The real value of this book will not come from merely reading it but from talking through the questions at the ends of chapters, using the knowledge you've gained to enrich your discussion. One of my favorite things about teaching college students is dialogue because it helps them develop their own perspectives, not simply memorize and repeat mine. In a class session in which thoughtful questions are posed, I sometimes see students wrinkle their eyebrows in thought, ask additional questions, and point out flaws in my own thinking. They are working to learn and find their own answers, becoming active learners rather than passive recipients of data. My hope is that this book will function similarly and serve as a pathway for couples to gain knowledge about sexuality and contraception, to sharpen their abilities to think ethically, and to make well-informed decisions together. This book will be helpful for engaged and married couples as well as for the friends, family members, and church leaders who support them. I encourage you to read it with pencil in hand, taking notes and writing down questions to pursue with your spouse, friend, healthcare provider, or pastor.

Despite living in a culture in which media inundates us with sexual talk and images, men and women still struggle to talk together intimately and honestly about their sexual lives. Before the birth control pill was developed, men played an integral role in pregnancy avoidance. In fact, male participation was essential for most methods, which included withdrawal, periodic abstinence, diaphragms, and condoms. Since the pill became available in the early 1960s, however, pregnancy avoidance has become invisible to many men because women frequently control their fertility by themselves. Too often men push women to make these choices alone, saying, "It's your body, and you should choose the method you are comfortable with." It *is* the woman's body, and she *should* find a method that is comfortable for her, but the consequences of contraceptive use—either avoided pregnancies or unintended pregnancies—are experienced by both men and women. Knowledge of fertility and contraception helps men to shoulder responsibility by enabling them to ask better questions and play a complementary role in decision making.

Examples from the developing world show that male involvement in family planning education increases and influences the rate of contraceptive use.[6] When Colombian men became involved

15

in family planning services, it benefited their marriages and their wives. Husbands listened more to their wives' health concerns, and they began to take their wives' ideas about family planning and childcare into stronger consideration. An international development group says when men share responsibility for family planning, the result is healthier marriages, better care for children, decreased rates of sexually transmitted diseases, and greater respect for women.[7]

Sexual intimacy is one of God's good gifts, shared between spouses again and again in the course of a marriage. Caring for this gift throughout a lifetime takes time, honesty, vulnerability, intimacy, and patience. And making wise choices about birth control is a large part of caring for the gift of sex. As with other decisions a married couple faces, good birth control decisions require ongoing conversation and prayer.

Part 1

Beginning the Conversation

1

Birth Control

An Important Issue for Christians

I intend to live according to not just what *I* believe, or have "been led to do," but what is in harmony with God's design, plan, love, life—the Bible, the church, and historic Christian teaching.

Aimee, age 33

Stand at the crossroads, and look, and ask for the ancient paths, where the good way lies; and walk in it, and find rest for your souls.

Jeremiah 6:16

We each make millions of decisions each day, many of them intuitive and unconscious: to get out of bed, eat certain foods, go to work, and interact with friends and family. Most of these decisions are not burdensome or time-consuming because they are established cultural patterns—behaviors that seem less like choices and more like normal daily life. Brushing your teeth or wearing shoes, for example, hardly seem like choices because everyone (that is, everyone like you!) does them. That's culture—patterns of living and thinking that people share with those around them. Much of the time culture shapes human thought and behavior in ways that are helpful, but cultures sometimes offer scant or even harmful guidance. For post-Enlightenment cultures, especially in the West, cultural norms surrounding sexuality, marriage, and relationships lead people in destructive directions. It is important for the believer to critically engage the culture, discerning what is good and what is not.

Christians have responded to the rapidly changing sexual norms of modern culture in various ways. A broad Christian consensus has persisted regarding the value of marriage, the impropriety of sex outside of marriage, and the evil of abortion, but modern Christians have not agreed about the morality of contraception. Our framework for making birth control choices begins by gathering insights from fellow believers who have thought deeply and Christianly about these matters.[1]

Some Christians Approve Modern Birth Control

Long before modern contraceptive technologies were developed, humans controlled fertility by various means including herbs, delayed marriage, withdrawal, and infanticide. Throughout Christian history women have regulated their fertility with the help of midwives and herbalists, and while Christian leaders sometimes condemned and sometimes affirmed these practices, for a long time no official or widely enforced church policies were in place. In the United States, Christian regulation of contraception and abortion became more stringent only after the development of modern science.

For much of the nation's history, American Christians limited their fertility in various ways, few of which were vigorously condemned by either Protestant or Catholic authorities. Infanticide and late-term abortions were condemned, but women were allowed to "regulate menstruation" to the point of "quickening." In other words, women could drink herbal poisons or otherwise induce menstruation in the early weeks of pregnancy. Church authorities back then did not think this was abortion because they and everyone believed life began when a woman could feel fetal movement, roughly fourteen weeks into pregnancy. As scientific understandings of reproduction became culturally dominant, nineteenth-century Christians responded by condemning any form of abortion, including menstrual induction after the beginning of pregnancy. Several methods of preventing conception were available, however, and continued to be widely used, including condoms, pessaries (similar to diaphragms), sponges, withdrawal, douches, and the rhythm method.[2]

In the mid–nineteenth century, activists in industrializing nations crusaded against many social ills, including prostitution, alcoholism, child labor abuses, overcrowding in cities, and obscenity. Anthony Comstock, a representative of the Society for the Suppression of Vice, lobbied New York State (and later the federal government) to pass new obscenity laws. These laws forbade the distribution of obscene materials, which contraceptive information was deemed to be, through the postal or customs systems.[3] Passed in 1873 as federal legislation applying to the District of Columbia and federal territories, the so-called "Comstock Law" provided a model for states that passed similar laws.

The Comstock laws severely limited access to contraceptive information. In addition, they created a public perception that contraception was obscene. Comstock himself equated contraceptives with pornography: "If you open the door to anything, the filth will all pour in and the degradation of youth will follow. . . . If you turn loose the passions and break down the fear [of pregnancy], you bring worse disaster than the war [World War I]. [Contraception] would debase sacred things, break down the health of women and disseminate a greater curse than the plagues and diseases of Europe."[4] Unfortunately, this view still persists; birth control is sometimes viewed "as something stealthy . . . that had at least better be kept strictly private."[5]

The American birth control movement, developed as a response to the Comstock laws, tried to recover the contraceptive freedom

21

women had lost. Margaret Sanger, a nurse in New York City, was troubled by the health and economic trauma that accompanied frequent pregnancies among low-income women. She often told the story of Sadie Sachs, a young married woman whom Sanger assisted after a botched abortion. Sachs later died after another attempted abortion. Sanger saw the physical harm that came to poorly nourished women after seven, eight, or even twelve pregnancies and the drastic measures women employed to avoid pregnancies. She became convinced that birth control would enhance women's health, making them better mothers and wives and thereby improving the lives of children as well. She thought "contraceptives would transform the status of married women from that of mere breeding machines to that of human beings with some measure of control over their biological destiny."[6] She opened a birth control clinic in New York City in 1916 and was immediately charged with being a "public nuisance." Intensive legal struggles lasted several years, and this prompted a stronger organization of procontraception activists.

These political and social controversies forced Christians to develop positions on contraception. Protestant denominations dealt with the issue of contraception in various ways, some at the congregational level, others in informal ways. The Anglican church had a more formal process for negotiating important issues, and it provides insight into Protestant reasoning on contraception.

Every ten years the bishops of the Anglican Church meet to discuss issues of importance to the church. This conference passes resolutions and declares statements, and its authority is significant in the life of individual congregations. In 1908 the Lambeth Conference condemned contraception, stating it defeated a primary aim of marriage, caused mental stress, and weakened character by encouraging irresponsibility.[7] The conference confirmed this stance in 1920 with the following statement: "We utter an emphatic warning against the use of unnatural means for the avoidance of conception, together with the grave dangers—physical, moral and religious—thereby incurred, and against the evils with which the extension of such use threatens the race."[8] The

1920 conference also affirmed the Comstock laws and the equating of contraception with obscenity, suggesting that bishops and active Christians should pressure authorities to remove "such incentives to vice as indecent literature, suggestive plays and films, the open or secret sale of contraceptives, and the continued existence of brothels."[9]

The 1920s saw an increase in birth control activism, which resulted in the easing of Comstock law enforcement and the eventual abolition of these laws state by state.[10] Despite its previous condemnations, the 1930 Lambeth Conference affirmed the use of contraception, though only under certain circumstances and after much debate and controversy. Following is a statement from the 1930 Lambeth Conference resolution regarding "The Life and Witness of the Christian Community — Marriage and Sex":

> Where there is clearly felt moral obligation to limit or avoid parenthood, the method must be decided on Christian principles. The primary and obvious method is complete abstinence from intercourse (as far as may be necessary) in a life of discipline and self-control lived in the power of the Holy Spirit. Nevertheless in those cases where there is such a clearly felt moral obligation to limit or avoid parenthood, and where there is a morally sound reason for avoiding complete abstinence, the Conference agrees that other methods may be used, provided that this is done in the light of the same Christian principles. The Conference records its strong condemnation of the use of any methods of conception control from motives of selfishness, luxury, or mere convenience.[11]

This resolution passed by a vote of 193 to 67, but it generated much discussion and dissent within and beyond the Anglican Church. Many Anglican theologians continued to condemn contraception well into the 1950s, and some maintain this stance today. In 1988 Anglican priest Alan Wilkinson wrote that with the acceptance of contraception, the church had caved in and followed culture's increasing individualism and sexual permissiveness, losing credibility as an independent moral authority. "Christians in all Churches," wrote Wilkinson, "simply exercised their own individual judgment about sexual issues, in the light of current attitudes in society and whatever they happened to know and accept of the Christian tradition."[12]

Despite such concerns, other Protestant denominations followed the example of the Anglican Church. In 1931 the majority of a committee of the Federal Council of Churches (a forerunner to the National Council of Churches) endorsed the "careful and restrained" use of birth control by married people.[13] The Anglican Church insisted, however, that contraceptive decisions not be made lightly, and the Federal Council of Churches expressed concern about evils that might stem from the use of contraceptives, such as extramarital sex. The council affirmed value in sex apart from procreation, asserting that motive, not method, is what made contraception good or bad. According to the council, if a couple avoids children in order to accumulate wealth, enjoy an easier life, or maintain a convenient existence, the couple is misusing contraception, while conditions such as financial instability or declining maternal health are moral grounds for the use of contraception.

Some Christians Reject Modern Birth Control

In contrast, the Catholic Church developed and maintained an anticontraceptive position in the twentieth century. Prior to the twentieth century, Catholic theologians sometimes commented on contraception, but their thought was not developed to the point of dogma, as on more central issues such as the Trinity or the resurrection. The 1922 *Catholic Encyclopedia Supplement* was one of the first strident condemnations of birth control, warning that contraception causes physical and moral disorders including tumors, sterility, loss of self-respect, infidelity, and divorce. It states that women who use contraception mistake "the conditions of a prostitute for those of married life."[14]

A benchmark event came with the publication of the papal encyclical *Casti Connubii* (Christian Marriage) in 1930. In the same year that the Lambeth Conference affirmed contraception, the Catholic Church rejected it. Pope Pius XI acknowledged that many Catholics were practicing contraception but stated the church must decry this "new and utterly perverse morality" in order to "keep the flock committed to Our care from poisoned pastures."[15] This encyclical provided precedent for *Humanae Vitae,* the most recent encyclical to directly address birth control.

Some Catholic scientists helped develop the birth control pill, seeing it as the most natural and therefore the most acceptable form of contraception. Unlike condoms, diaphragms, or sponges, which involve inserting foreign objects into the body and into the sexual act, the pill seemed to work with the body's natural processes. In 1967 the Majority Report of the Papal Birth Control Commission concurred, advising the pope to affirm contraception.[16] Pope Paul VI disagreed, however, and in opposition to these advisors reaffirmed *Casti Connubii* and issued the 1968 encyclical *Humanae Vitae.* While many Catholics agreed with the pope, others immediately criticized his position. Rather than describe all the details of this conflict, it best suits our purposes to relate some of the pope's concerns. Many Christians, even those who disagree with the pope's unequivocal condemnation of contraception, consider seriously his moral cautions.

The pope described four "grave consequences" of contraception in *Humanae Vitae,* each of which are worthy of consideration by Christians who use birth control. The first is that contraception opens up a road to marital infidelity and a widespread lowering of morality. Indeed, many scholars agree that "the contraceptive revolution moved hand in hand with changes in both sexual behavior and attitudes."[17] After World War I, American youth developed patterns of nonmarital relations that later were known as "dating," and the physicality of dating increased throughout the twentieth century. In 1962, for example, Helen Gurley Brown authored a popular book titled *Sex and the Single Girl: The Unmarried Woman's Guide to Men.* Brown assumed her young women readers had access to contraception as she advised them to seek affairs, develop their sexual abilities, and make flirting and sexual suggestiveness part of their dress and conduct. She mocked chaste women, asking the question, "Is there anything particularly attractive about a thirty-four-year-old virgin?"[18] Many social, economic, and political changes impacted American notions of sex throughout the twentieth century, but contraception provided an essential tool for sexual "liberation."

Second, the pope expressed a concern for the marital relationship. He worried that "the man, growing used to the employment of anticonceptive practices, may finally lose respect for the woman and, no longer caring for her physical and psychological equilibrium, may come to the point of considering her as a mere instrument of selfish enjoyment."[19] Natural family planning (the "child spacing method" approved by the Catholic Church) requires a man to respond to a woman's cycles, while contraception allows a man to demand "that their wives be ready for sex at all times."[20] Marital sex-on-demand may be an extreme case, but contraception does allow men to distance themselves from the consequences of their sexual actions. People who use contraception may also develop a way of life that prioritizes wealth or leisure, and these people may view a pregnancy (especially an unexpected one) as an inconvenience or intrusion.

Third, contraceptive technology places a "dangerous weapon" in the hands of governments. Governments or other powerful groups may coerce populations into using contraception for purposes of genocide, population reduction, or enhancing manipulative control. Charles Curran, a Catholic scholar who dissented from *Humanae Vitae,* nonetheless agreed with each of the pope's concerns, particularly the danger of the strong using contraceptive technology to control the weak: "The poor in the country, women in general, and the poor nations of the world have all been victims of the contraceptive technology of the powerful."[21] Indeed, by the mid–twentieth century at least seventeen American states passed laws that allowed for the involuntary sterilization of mentally retarded, insane, and other "undesirable" people. The last of these laws remained in effect until the 1970s. Numerous nations, including Denmark, Sweden, and most notably Nazi Germany used sterilization and sometimes euthanasia to eliminate "unfit" populations. Another powerful example is when the United States government authorized medical testing of the birth control pill in Puerto Rico. Thousands of Puerto Rican women were, without their knowledge, given experimental doses of the pill, and as a result many experienced temporary and permanent sterilization or painful side effects, and some even died.[22]

Lastly, *Humanae Vitae* warns against self-delusion. Contraception can lead people to believe falsely that they can control their own lives, disregarding the natural limitations of both the body and technology. Technologies contain both promises and pitfalls, many of which are unforeseeable. A user of a technology must know its purpose to assess whether it is leading forward or astray.[23] Birth control may allow a family to procreate responsibly and care for children, and it may enhance a couple's intimate relationship by reducing fear of pregnancy. On the other hand, it may allow a woman to make contraceptive decisions without consulting her husband, or it could enable a couple to disregard God's plan for their family and rely on technology alone to control their future.

An Important Issue for Christians

Today, many Protestants are simply grateful they aren't Catholic when it comes to birth control. Many Catholics, despite a love for the church, practice birth control in defiance of church policy. One study found that in the early 1980s, 76 percent of American Catholics practiced birth control, and 94 percent of that group practiced methods condemned by the church (i.e., methods other than natural family planning).[24]

As individual Christians make personal choices about birth control, they may benefit from the insights and struggles of fellow Christians in various times and historic traditions. From Anglicans we learn to examine motives. Children should not be avoided for the sake of material luxury, selfishness, or mere convenience. From Catholics we learn to consider the potential negative outcomes of our decisions, personal and societal. Both traditions emphasize the primary importance of choosing a good spouse, acknowledging that a good marriage provides the best home for children. They also emphasize that regardless of the contraceptive method used, pregnancy is always a possibility in a sexual relationship.

Procontraception Christians argue that birth control is generally good for people. Women's health, life opportunities, and economic security improve when people can develop themselves without the physical burden of frequent pregnancies. Contraception improves marriages as couples are free to express sexual love and intimacy without fear of pregnancy. According to pro-contraception Christians, "to free human beings from physical necessity and to give them greater control and responsibility enhances the reality of the human."[25]

These positive aspects, however, cannot neatly cancel out the negative implications of contraception. Despite the benefits it bestows, contraceptive technology poses moral dilemmas to love, sex, marriage, and parenting. In addition, contraceptive technologies can cause harmful side effects even as they accomplish beneficial ends. Lastly, contraceptive technologies are susceptible to abuse on both personal and societal levels, as the strong may use technologies to oppress the weak.

For many people the harms of contraception outweigh the benefits. These people may use natural methods or refuse to regulate their reproduction at all. For others, the harms are held in tension with the benefits. These people may use contraception but with a wary eye toward ways in which it can harm their marriage or health. Such people often keep an eye out for ways governments or other powers are abusing their chosen technology. Making birth control choices in an ethical way requires us to consider both the good and the bad in the technologies we use and to be aware of the broader social effects of our choices.

2

Making Wise Choices
about Birth Control

C hristian advice about sexuality often comes in the form
of rules. "No sex before marriage" and "no sex outside of marriage" are two that come quickly to mind.
As any dating person knows, the "no sex before marriage"
rule is of limited use when it comes to making choices about
touch in a romantic relationship. Rules are good for defining
the lines that should not be crossed, but they aren't as helpful when it comes to the ambiguities of real-life relationships.

In addition, when it comes to contraceptive decision making, people often invoke rules that offer only limited guidance.
Gary, a fifty-year-old married man, said, "I would say anything
that destroys the — I don't know the biological term — but once
the egg and sperm are united, anything that would destroy that,
I would say is unethical. But I'm not opposed to any [other]
method, as long as it's not harmful to anyone's health." Angela,
a twenty-year-old married woman, said, "I guess the only

method I can think of [that Christians should avoid] is the morning-after pill, or abortion." When facing numerous options, the "no abortion" rule, like the "no sex" rule for dating couples, is helpful only to a point. It rules out abortion, but what about all the other ways to prevent conception? A couple's individual situation, personal health histories, goals for the future, and financial and personal maturity all factor into their decisions. Contraceptive needs change over time as well, so a couple that at one point avoids pregnancy may later space children out with contraception and eventually end their reproductive capacity altogether. We need more than a few rules to make these decisions. We need an ethical framework that guides decision making throughout changing life circumstances.

King David wrote a psalm about the peace and rest that come from living right with God. It begins, "Protect me, O God, for in you I take refuge. I say to the LORD, 'You are my Lord; I have no good apart from you.'" David wanted to do more than follow God's rules. He wanted to enjoy the safety and good of living in God's pleasure. He gives thanks for God's help, stating, "The boundary lines have fallen for me in pleasant places" (Psalm 16:1–2, 6). For me, this psalm conjures images of a person enjoying the land he owns. The boundary lines of his property give him ample space to build a home, grow food, and support animals — in short, to live a fulfilling life. Likewise, we may praise the Lord for the pleasant boundaries he has given us — space and freedom to enjoy life in God's world.

Boundaries rather than rules give both great freedom and great responsibility to the Christian. How may we wisely exercise freedom in the area of birth control and live within the pleasant boundaries given to us by God? There are many ways to consider this question, and this chapter develops one model that may be helpful. We will consider the biblical theme of *shalom*, or peace, by exploring the relationships that ought to affect our birth control decisions as well as the blessings and harms that may result from our choices. We will draw on insights from both Protestants and Catholics, and we will borrow from medical experts who have researched how people make birth control choices. The questions at the end of this chapter may guide your conversation and reflection about which options are best for you.

Right Relationships

Shalom, which in addition to "peace" can be translated "reconciliation," "righteousness," and "justice," is a foundational biblical theme that describes the nature of God's kingdom and the ideal of the Christian life. Paul describes Christ's work as reconciliation that ultimately brings all creation together in harmony and peace: "For in [Christ] all the fullness of God was pleased to dwell, and through him God was pleased to reconcile to himself all things, whether on earth or in heaven, by making peace through the blood of his cross" (Colossians 1:19). Isaiah describes *shalom* as the distinguishing characteristic of God's kingdom. Jesus will bring the kingdom, and "he will faithfully bring forth justice" to the earth (Isaiah 42:3). In John 14 Jesus promised his disciples that after he left the earth, the Holy Spirit would remain to comfort and lead them by the Spirit's peace.

Sometimes peace is poorly understood as merely the absence of war or conflict, though certainly the absence of war is no small thing. The medical equivalent is viewing physical health as merely the absence of disease. A person can live with poor nutrition, lousy exercise habits, and a foul disposition, yet be free of disease. This person may be deemed healthy but only in a very limited sense. While peace does involve the absence of negative qualities such as hardship, conflict, death, and a troubled mind, this is only a partial definition of peace. Peace is also the presence of well-being, harmony, and rest—the good life described by King David in Psalm 16. The kingdom of God is characterized by *shalom* in all aspects of life—economics, politics, culture, family, and personal life. In terms of reproductive health, peace includes enjoying sexual and intimate relationships and experiencing the joy of living one's sexual life fully before God.

The model I will use for discussing *shalom*, therefore, will be that of a couple or an individual who lives rightly with four beings or entities—God, self, each other, and the world God made. One may refer to this model when considering career choices, parenting, diet, or any other aspect of life. In terms of contraception, however, the model helps couples realize that a wise decision comes from being at peace with God, their individual selves, each other, and their contraceptive method. At the very least, contraception should not do harm in any of these relationships, and if our goal is the fullest sense of *shalom,* we should hope for contraception to promote goodness and peace.

Relationship with God

God blessed us with the gift of bodies, so caring for our bodies is an important part of our relationship with God — the first of our four key relationships. When we avoid pregnancy, we rely upon human-created technologies and knowledge to influence the way our bodies work. Similarly, when we use seatbelts or refrigeration or sunscreen, we rely upon the products of human ingenuity to preserve and enhance our quality of life. One reason Christians disagree about contraception is because some believe it strips away our reliance on God, making us self-sufficient and more apt to reject God's plan for our families. When Anglicans first affirmed birth control in 1930, they said the use of contraceptive technology did not necessarily reduce our trust in God. It may or may not harm our relationship with God, according to the Anglican leaders, depending on the motives of the user. A couple should ask, "Why are we avoiding pregnancy?" Desiring a particular income, lifestyle, measure of convenience, or physical appearance, couples may use contraception to hold more and more control in their own hands. On the other hand, couples may use contraception to add stability and maturity to their marriage before having children or to remain child free in order to serve God in other ways. Considering motive may allow for the preservation and enhancement of a couple's relationship with God.

A second aspect of our relationship with God is whether or not a contraceptive method is wrong in and of itself. Among Christians who allow for the use of contraception, very few question the morality of behavioral methods, barrier methods, or permanent methods. Natural family planning, condoms, sterilization, and other methods are viewed as relatively simple technologies that rarely harm the life of a man or woman and do not harm a fetus. Angela, a twenty-year-old married woman, said, "There is always the classic condom. This form of birth control . . . is highly uncontroversial. It is seen in most circles as being morally correct and serves its purpose." Hormonal methods and IUDs are much more controversial because some view them as abortifacients (agents that cause abortion). Most of the time these methods prevent ovulation or fertilization, but sometimes they may prevent a fertilized egg from implanting in the uterus. (This issue is covered in detail in chapters 12 and 15.) Many Christians say contraception becomes morally wrong when it is used to terminate a life that has already begun.

Mary, a thirty-two-year-old married woman, seems uncomfortable with the issue: "I know the pill can sometimes prevent a fertilized egg from implanting, but I really don't want to get pregnant. I just don't tell my husband how it works, because if he knew, he wouldn't let me use it." The abortive effects of hormonal methods and IUDs are debatable and complex, yet the matter is of utmost importance for many Christians.

Relationship with Self

The second key relationship to consider is a person's relationship with self. A wise contraceptive decision will, at the very least, preserve a clear conscience and a healthy body. At best, it may enhance a person's self-respect, self-knowledge, and physical health.

Self-observation methods offer the most potential for enhancing self-knowledge, because with them a couple learns a lot about fertility and the female body. Jane, a twenty-nine-year-old married woman, said, "Fertility awareness is amazing! I know so much more about my body, my cycle, and my moods. It has helped me care for my body and my health better." Condoms and male sterilization offer potential for men to shoulder the responsibility for contraception, and some men express gratitude for the opportunity to take this role in their relationship. Hormonal methods, the IUD, and sterilization may preserve a clear conscience, and sometimes they even enhance health.

Safety is a major consideration in birth control decisions and is an important part of a person's relationship with self. The side effects of behavioral and barrier methods are usually minor, and this is a strong advantage for many users. The side effects of hormonal methods and the IUD are sometimes irritating and even dangerous. Dale, a twenty-seven-year-old man, said, "[Linda, my wife] took the pill because I guess that's what everybody does, and it was a real time of turmoil for her emotions and her body chemistry. She was a different person. I think [it was] just the way the chemicals made her react physiologically and also emotionally, and that type of thing. We just said, 'Forget this, it's not worth it.'" On the other hand, Marcy, a twenty-year-old married woman, said, "I think the pill is a marvelous invention that allows women to marry and not have to run around barefoot and pregnant for the majority of their God-given lives!" Linda and Marcy had very different experiences with hormonal contraception, and while one found it unbearable, the other found it to be a great blessing. Sometimes contraceptive methods bring even more blessing in their noncontraceptive effects. Some women use the pill, for example, even when they are not sexually active to manage acne or menstrual problems. These blessings are also important in promoting a healthy relationship with the self.

Each time we accept medical care we face questions of stewardship. Are the benefits of this intervention worth the risks? Am I caring for my body or being reckless with it? People vary in their assessments of risk and their expectations of benefits, as they also vary in the ways their bodies respond to various technologies. Fortunately, with most methods it is possible to switch when side effects become unbearable. It is not uncommon for a couple to try three or four or even more birth control methods in the course of a marriage.

Relationship with Spouse

The third relationship is the marital relationship. Each type of contraception may bless or harm a marriage in various ways. When a couple feels confident of their contraceptive choice, birth control can free them to enjoy sexual intimacy without fear of pregnancy. If a couple shares the responsibility for contraception, this may help them share responsibility in other parts of life as well.

Behavioral methods involve communication and cooperation between spouses. Spouses talk about whether or not the woman is fertile and negotiate expressions of intimacy during fertile times. Brian, a forty-year-old, said, "My wife and I decided to practice natural family planning. . . . We have never regretted it. It certainly has aided us both in respecting one another's bodies. And it builds self-control into marriage." Behavioral methods may harm a marriage, however, if both people are not committed to it. If one resists abstinence or the use of barriers during fertile times, the method can cause conflict and resentment.

Barrier methods may be a wise choice because they are low-tech and carry few health risks, but some couples find the use of a barrier to be an interruption to foreplay, intercourse, or sexual spontaneity. Sterilization terminates the reproductive potential of a sexual union, and this also may bless or harm a couple. Getting a vasectomy may be the first way that a husband shares responsibility for contraception. Michael, a thirty-eight-year-old married man, boasted, "We've had four children. There will be no more! You can be sure *I've* taken care of that!" Sterilization may harm a marriage, however, if one person feels coerced into the procedure and later regrets the choice.

Relationship with Technology

The final relationship is with the chosen technology, part of the world God made. Being at peace with the technology we choose may be difficult because a technology may have unintended and unforeseen consequences that are far removed from the individual user. For example, the legalization of birth control in the United States allowed many women to improve their health and control their reproduction, but birth control was also used by eugenicists to control the reproduction of people deemed "unfit" for society. It was forced on working-class and poor women, and thousands of mentally impaired people were sterilized without their permission. These eugenics policies played out in the United States, many European countries, Japan, and reached their peak in Nazi Germany.

Even today foreign aid is sometimes contingent upon the use of family planning programs, and some see these policies as global-scale control of the weak by the politically and economically strong. Some African Americans continue to criticize hormonal contraceptive methods or at least highlight their potential for both liberation and oppression, because the pill has been used by eugenicists and other family planning organizations in "deliberate campaigns to limit black fertility" throughout the twentieth century. Similar critiques are made of some internationally funded family planning interventions in Brazil, Puerto Rico, and much of Africa.[1]

In *Humanae Vitae*, Pope Paul VI warned about the possibility of contraceptive technologies being used as a weapon by the strong against the weak. Some users of contraception speak of feeling somehow connected to atrocities that are facilitated by the method they have chosen. While individual users are not personally responsible for these abuses of power, we still might consider the global implications of the technologies we use. In prayerful consideration, you may find that you don't want to use a technology that has harmed others, or you may find ways of compensating, however indirectly, for the harms caused to others by technologies that benefit you. For example, if your chosen contraceptive technology has harmed people in the developing world, you could financially support or pray for an organization that helps people in those areas.

Another aspect of being at peace with contraceptive technology is simply being at peace with using medical technology in general. Michael, a fifty-five-year-old, said about his wife, "Her family was antimedication as much as possible. Don't take any medicine unless you're really sick. So being from that kind of environment, it seemed that we should just use condoms." On the other hand, Richelle, a thirty-four-year-old married woman, said about reproductive technologies, "Sign me up! I want a doctor who is aggressive with infertility treatments." Some people are generally comfortable with medical interventions and some are more cautious. This gut-level approach to technology is a meaningful starting point for considering various technologies.

These four relationships—with God, self, spouse, and technology—offer rich substance for reflection, study, prayer, and dialogue. Enjoying God's *shalom* in life's key relationships is not a goal to achieve. Rather, it is a lifelong process because relationships, priorities, and needs change over time. Lewis and Meg, a married couple in their thirties, used natural family planning to space out the births of their children for the first several years of their marriage. They believed in its philosophy and felt that it honored God and each other. After having two children, Meg found that it was difficult to chart her fertility symptoms daily while attending to her energetic toddlers, so they began using a diaphragm. A different couple, Steve and Cheryl, now in their forties, used an IUD for several years until Cheryl unexpectedly became pregnant with their first child. Her pregnancy was high risk, and she nearly died in childbirth. After their child was born, Steve decided to have a vasectomy to protect his wife's health from future pregnancies. Paying close attention to the relationships that really matter helped guide these couples' decisions through major life changes.

This model of peace is not a license to be selfish. For example, a woman cannot enjoy peace with her husband if she deceives him about her use of birth control, whether to achieve or avoid a pregnancy. A woman cannot enjoy peace with herself if a contraceptive technology creates unbearable physical side effects. This model does, however, allow for personal freedom. In my life, for example, I was unable to resolve the moral questions associated with hormonal contraception and was uncomfortable with possible side effects, so I could not use these methods in peace. Technological sophistication and moral complexity often go hand in hand, so for me the more technologically simple the method, the more peace I found with myself and with God.

This is certainly not true for all Christians. Some are able to find peace with a method that another Christian finds unacceptable. Jeremy, a nineteen-year-old single man, discovered a wise insight: "I respect and value the choices that my immediate family has made concerning birth control, and I recognize that it is difficult for me to come to conclusions that could alienate me from them morally." He tried to reach a position that would please his parents but ultimately came to a different, yet respectful conclusion. Couples should talk and work together to refine their choices and to discern the good boundaries that God has set. Contraception is not directly addressed in Scripture, so we need humility as we attempt to apply biblical insights to our contemporary world, leaving space for the Holy Spirit to give and withhold peace.

The Best Birth Control?

Beth and Scott, an engaged couple in my fertility awareness course, reviewed a pamphlet containing information about fifteen contraceptive options. Scott said, "I don't like any of these! All have aspects I don't like." Scott was pointing out the truth that all birth control methods involve trade-offs. For example, the pill may be higher in effectiveness and more convenient, but a woman who uses this method may experience irritating side effects, or her insurance company may not cover the expense. Condoms may offer protection against STDs, but interrupt foreplay. Self-observation methods may help women avoid hormonal side effects, but they take time and energy to learn. The best birth control won't be perfect, but it will maximize benefits and minimize drawbacks.

Researchers have learned that several factors influence contraceptive decisions, including stage of life, culture, and priorities. Understanding these factors will help you choose which birth control method is right for you and your spouse.

Stage of Life

The "seven contraceptive ages of women" are: birth to puberty, puberty to marriage, marriage to first child, during breast feeding, family spacing after breast feeding, after the last child, family complete, and premenopausal.[2] In some of these stages (birth to puberty, for instance), caring for reproductive health does not involve contraception. Rather, reproductive health in childhood involves the parents safeguarding a child's health for the future. For stages that do involve contraception, different methods are more workable for various stages. It is important to recognize your "contraceptive age" as well as your hopes for the future with respect to reproduction. Transitions between stages and other life changes often mark times of contraceptive decision making — the beginning of sexual experience, after an unexpected pregnancy, career change, after a planned birth, when the family is complete, or when there are problems with a method currently in use.

Culture

Culture is the second factor influencing method choice. Research has shown that couples in Zimbabwe, other parts of Africa, Turkey, and Bangladesh rarely use contraception until after the birth of a first child or until the family is complete. Ruth, an African woman, said, "It is extremely necessary to have a first child before a couple contracepts. Why would one practice family planning if one does not even have a family?"[3] In contrast, couples in the United States often use contraception before marriage and during the early years of marriage to prevent pregnancy and delay their family.

Cultural norms surrounding male and female behaviors are also important. In some cultures, including sub-Saharan Africa, western Asia, and northern Africa, condom use is associated with prostitutes and is not considered proper for marriage.[4] In India contraception is frequently used to end childbearing after a family is complete, and women often choose sterilization.[5]

In the United States contraceptive use varies significantly by subculture. European American women are most likely to use the pill, and African American and Native American women are more likely to use Norplant (see chapter 13) than European American or Asian American women.[6] These differences reflect complex cultural processes of information-sharing and social norms among various groups of Americans, and they reinforce the notion that contraception is not a one-size-fits-all decision.

Priorities

A third factor is priorities. Couples prioritize different aspects of contraception and then make trade-offs to achieve their highest priorities. A survey of U.S. women identified the following as characteristics of their ideal birth control method:[7]

- easy to use
- safe
- effective
- few or no side effects
- natural
- nonhormonal
- taken monthly
- allows user to get pregnant soon after stopping use

You may define other characteristics important to you, including positive impact on relationship with spouse, consistency with religious beliefs, cost, and others.

Working with Health-Care Providers

Because contraception involves a person's worldview, ongoing personal journey, and body, it is important to have the right health-care provider. Health-care providers shoulder important responsibilities that have an impact on your life, so search out excellent care. If a health-care provider devalues your perspective or does not answer your questions, do not hesitate to find another.

Increasingly, people find that their health-care providers do not spend adequate time explaining diagnoses, procedures, and options. This reality and the proliferation of medical information in self-help books and on the Internet have profoundly altered the relationship between patient and doctor. More than ever patients research and negotiate their health care and no longer accept medical authority as absolute. In 1973 a medical writer predicted, "[Patients] will not revere the physician as the mediator of special knowledge. Patients will quite likely regard themselves as fellow-citizens demanding technical information."[8] More recently, the Georgetown University Institute for Reproductive Health described the same shift: "Increasingly the patient has moved from being a passive participant of care to a client or consumer of care who weighs alternatives, seeks second opinions, and assumes responsibility for prevention through self-examination, diet, exercise, early treatment, and accident prevention measures."[9]

Even if your chosen method does not require a doctor's visit, it is likely that caring for your reproductive health will involve medical consultation at various times in your life. You and your health-care provider should work together to promote *shalom* in your reproductive health.

What Your Health-Care Provider Can Do

Provide contraceptive counseling. Health-care providers should ask questions to determine which contraceptives are good options for you. Make sure they know your medical history, current medications, sexual activity, and plans for future pregnancies.

Prescribe, fit, or inform. Some methods, including diaphragms, the pill, implants, injections, IUDs, and cervical caps, require medical assistance. Other methods, including condoms, spermicides, and self-observation methods, do not require medical assistance. Health-care providers can, however, answer questions about these methods as well. Again, if a health-care provider is not experienced with your method or pressures you to accept a certain method, find a new provider.

Provide adequate ongoing care. One reason for unintended pregnancy even when using highly effective methods, such as the pill, implants, or injections, is lack of follow-up care. Be sure that you understand the method's protocol and follow it precisely. Some methods require occasional visits for procedures such as new injections or removal of implants. Another reason for unintended pregnancy is that when a woman is dissatisfied with the side effects of a method, she may disregard the method and begin practicing contraception irregularly or not at all. If you experience unacceptable side effects, see a doctor immediately. A doctor may be able to identify serious health risks, alleviate your discomfort, or counsel you to use a different method.

What You Can Do

Develop an ethical framework for your sexual life. This book, together with your church and other spiritual resources, may help you develop a biblical worldview. Because the Christian way of life is distinct from that of the world, it is important for Christians to view the world through different lenses. Reflective decision making can help you keep your sexual and contraceptive decisions in harmony with your Christian worldview.

Communicate with your spouse. I know I've said this before, and you can be sure I'll say it again! The importance of communication between spouses cannot be stressed enough. Communication will help you make a wise decision, change your minds later if necessary, and achieve unity in this part of your life. Communication about birth control may also enhance dialogue about sex, intimacy, and vulnerability in marriage.

Take your birth control seriously. Contraceptive choices involve many aspects of life: your sexual past, your current situation, your hopes for the future, your physical health, and your expectations for effectiveness, safety, convenience, and cost. Considering these aspects carefully and discussing them with both your spouse and your health-care provider will help you make a well-informed decision.

Make a list of questions. Before visiting a doctor, write a list of questions. Health-care providers often do not have much time to spend with each patient, so writing your questions will help you recall them. Keep a running list of questions as you read this book and bring the appropriate ones to an office visit.

Follow your method's protocol. If your method comes in a package, the U.S. Food and Drug Administration (FDA) requires the manufacturer to include information about the product in an insert. Make sure that you read this important leaflet. You may also access information through product websites. For any kind of contraception, effectiveness relies heavily on you. Be sure that you understand your responsibilities with the method you choose. A method with a high effectiveness rate is effective only when used consistently and correctly.

The Importance of Communication

Todd, a twenty-seven-year-old married man, found that intimacy with his wife was enhanced when they discussed his wife's reproductive health and the method of contraception they had chosen: "Just because we're both aware of what the other person is thinking, it helps us talk about things a little more. It's helped me keep more attuned with her. . . . In today's society, sexual relationships are often selfishly motivated. I've really tried to make sure that in our marriage it's about putting her first, and putting the way she's feeling and how she's doing as some of the first priorities in our sexual relationship."

When Frank (thirty) and Bev (twenty-seven) talked about birth control, they learned more about how the other felt about their choice of contraception.

FRANK: The pill's nice. It's so convenient, so we don't have to worry. I don't have to worry about anything.
BEV: I have some sympathy for the women who say the pill puts responsibility completely on the woman. I don't mind it, but I can

BEGINNING THE CONVERSATION

kind of see where they're coming from. The responsibility is mine to remember it.

FRANK: You never told me this. You never tell me these things.

BEV: It really doesn't bother me.

FRANK: O.K.

BEV: But, like I said, if . . .

FRANK (interrupting): Apparently it does affect our relationship!

If, like Frank and Bev, you find that you are not in perfect agreement with your spouse, welcome to marriage! When disagreements arise, first listen with respect and then clarify points of disagreement. Perhaps you will come to agreement or perhaps the issue may be set aside for later discussion. If you are dating or engaged, it is essential to evaluate the importance of your differences. Ask yourself, "Could I live with this difference in my marriage even if it never gets resolved?" Some differences are dangerous to a marriage (e.g., when one person finds birth control to be morally unacceptable and the other thinks it is fine, or when one person wants children and the other does not). Do not assume that you or your partner will later have a change of mind. More often than not, what you see is what you get!

Questions for Conversation

Following is a list of questions that will help you and your spouse or fiancé(e) make wise choices about birth control. I encourage you to spend time together talking through these questions.

1. Do you want to have children? How many? When?

2. Why do you want to use birth control? Are you preventing pregnancy forever, delaying pregnancy for a while, or spacing children?

3. Do you have health concerns that may impact contraceptive choices? Do you have concerns about your fertility, sexually transmitted diseases, or other medical issues?

4. What do you believe about the purpose and meaning of sex?

5. What does your religious tradition say about sex and contraception? Do you agree or disagree?

6. What is important to you about birth control (e.g., effectiveness, ease of use, convenience, cost, safety, protection against sexually transmitted diseases)?

7. How concerned are you about an unexpected pregnancy? Rate your concern on a scale of one to ten (one meaning "No problem!" and ten meaning "This would be an emergency!"). What would happen if you became pregnant unexpectedly?

8. What is your general attitude toward medical technology? At what point do side effects become unbearable? At what point does technology become morally suspect?

9. What are your ideals for communicating with your spouse about sex and contraception? How have you worked toward these goals so far? How would you like your relationship to grow and improve in this area?

10. How does the man feel about his responsibility for contraception? How does the woman feel? What balance of male-female responsibility for contraception makes you comfortable?

11. What other questions do you want to discuss? Share them with each other.

3

The Birds, the Bees, and the Beginning of Life

Learning about sex is often awkward and embarrassing for students and their teachers. In my junior high instruction on breast self-exams, Mrs. Olson asked us to squeeze a synthetic breast to feel the lump. Students refused to squeeze, passing the plastic breast around the room in a red-faced game of hot potato. The next year, Mr. Gilmore, my biology teacher, said the state of Minnesota mandated him to teach sex education, but he didn't want to talk about it in front of the entire class. Students could come to his office outside of class to ask questions. I suspect this plan allowed him to evade the topic altogether!

Adolescents often learn about sex from peers and from "the talk" with their mothers (research shows that fathers rarely give the sex talk). The one-time birds-and-bees talk doesn't provide enough information or create a climate in which sexuality may be freely discussed. Also, it rarely gets beyond the issue of sexual intercourse, so contraception, AIDS, and sexually transmitted diseases are left unaddressed.[1] This means when adolescents become adults, they have misinformation or limited knowledge about sexuality, which makes them less comfortable discussing sex with *their* children, and so the pattern continues.

While it may seem that modern media-saturated people know everything about sex, we are for the most part merely taught to consume sexual images and laugh at sexual innuendo. Silence surrounds the real stuff of sex: relationships, intimacy, and intercourse with its blessings and complexities. Reviewing the birds and the bees (or learning it for the first time!) as an adult is a fascinating study that can debunk myths, increase self-appreciation, and enhance your ability to talk with and value your spouse. It's also the first step in making contraceptive choices. A family planning expert says, "To regulate your fertility, you first have to be aware of it. . . . Incorrect use or discontinuation of contraceptives is sometimes because of limited awareness of fertility."[2] When a couple understands fertility and conception, they are more likely to make an informed decision regarding contraception and to use it correctly and consistently.

So, where do babies come from? A pregnancy requires healthy sperm, a healthy egg, and fertile cervical fluid. If any of these are missing, conception cannot occur. Most birth control methods work by altering this equation in some way: preventing sperm and egg from meeting, inhibiting ovulation, changing the quality of cervical fluid, or altering the uterine lining to prevent implantation. It takes a fertile man and a fertile woman having sex during the woman's fertile time to make a baby. This chapter describes male and female fertility and the ways in which birth control intervenes in these processes.

Male Fertility

People joke that men think with their penises, but in truth the brain and penis *are* closely connected. At puberty, the pituitary gland sends a message to the testes telling them to make testosterone, the hormone that produces sperm as well as secondary sex characteristics including lowered voice and hair on the pubic area, chest, and face. As men will readily admit, the testes are

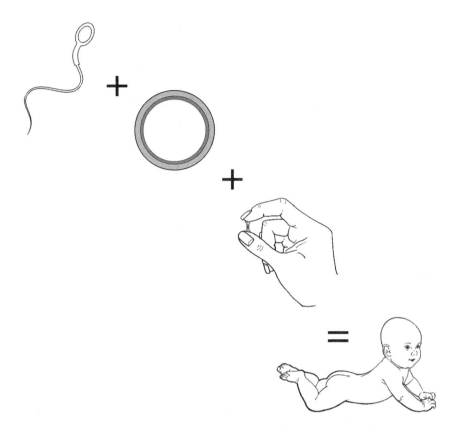

Fig. 3.1. The Pregnancy Equation. It takes healthy sperm, a healthy egg, and fertile cervical fluid to make a pregnancy.

sensitive and vulnerable, hanging behind the penis in sacs called scrotum. Sperm are manufactured in the testes, and their initial production requires a temperature that is three to four degrees below normal body temperature. The scrotum ensure this temperature by loosening the skin to hang low when a man is hot or by tightening and raising the scrotum close to the body when the man's temperature is cool. Penises and scrotums come in various sizes, but they all function the same way.[3]

Men produce an average of 200 million sperm per day. If each of his sperm reached a fertile egg, one man in one day could sire

49

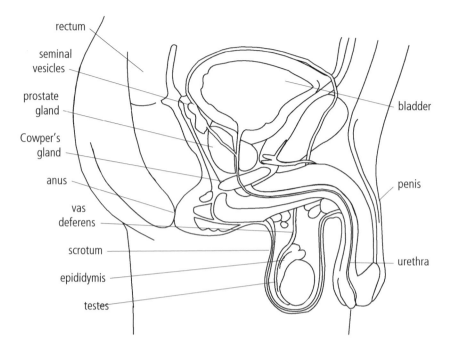

Fig. 3.2. Male Reproductive Anatomy.

enough children to double the population of Central America! The sperm move from the testes into the epididymis, a twenty-foot-long series of thin tubes that store and nurture young sperm. Sperm use these tubes like an Olympic pool for twelve days, perfecting their swimming technique and attaining fertilization maturity.

Sperm leave the man's body in ejaculatory fluid (also called semen), a mix of sperm, fluid from the seminal vesicles, and fluid from the prostate gland. Before ejaculation, the Cowper's gland releases a clear fluid designed to neutralize the acidity of the urethra and facilitate sperm movement. This pre-ejaculate comes out of the penis several minutes before ejaculation. Some people think this is because the man cannot control his ejaculation, but it actually is an essential step in the process toward ejaculation and cannot be predicted or controlled. It prepares the way for the sperm to survive and swim through the urethra during ejaculation. Pre-ejaculate contains no sperm or very few,

50

but a few sperm may be present from a previous ejaculation. At ejaculation sperm move from the epididymis into the vas deferens, a pair of tubes that carry sperm to the seminal vesicles. Sperm mix with fluids from the prostate gland and seminal vesicles, creating semen that moves into the passageway of the ejaculatory duct. It is then released through the urethra, bursting from the tip of the penis during ejaculation.

Women have a urethra for urination and a vagina for intercourse, but men use the urethra for both functions. Men cannot urinate during ejaculation because a muscular sphincter closes the opening of the bladder when the penis is engorged with blood during arousal. Fluid from the Cowper's gland flushes the urethra as well, preparing it to carry semen.

Male fertility is a force of nature! Men produce 100 to 500 million sperm per day, from puberty until age seventy or later. There are 150 to 400 million sperm in each ejaculate. In a friendly vaginal environment, sperm can survive up to five days awaiting ovulation and the opportunity to fertilize an egg. Consider the reproductive possibilities! The woman who best took advantage of these facts was the wife of Feodor Vassilyer, an eighteenth-century Russian peasant who bore sixty-nine children. In the twentieth century, Leontina Albina, of San Antonio, Chile, gave birth to her fifty-fifth (and last) baby in 1981.[4] If women's fertility were the same as men's, church nurseries would be bursting at the seams, stockholders in Babies R Us would be billionaires, and women would be very, very tired! Fortunately, male fertility is only one part of the story.

How Birth Control Intervenes in Male Fertility

At present, several methods of contraception are available for men. Men can participate in behavioral methods, including natural family planning, fertility awareness, and withdrawal. They also can alter their behavior in response to a woman's fertility (self-observation methods or Standard Days Method), or in response to their own fertility (withdrawal). These methods are

51

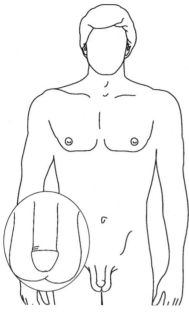

Behavioral Methods

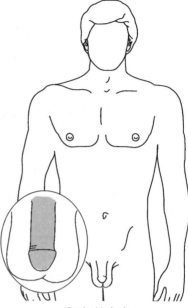

Barrier Methods

Shaded areas represent the part of body that is affected by a particular birth control method.

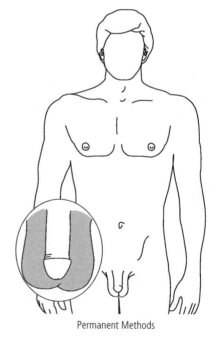

Permanent Methods

Fig. 3.3. How Birth Control Methods Affect the Male Body.

entirely noninvasive and do not affect the male reproductive system at all.

The other two methods of male contraception, condoms and sterilization, do impact the body. These methods are similar because they prevent sperm and egg from meeting but differ in how they do this. Condoms act as a barrier between sperm and egg, preventing them from meeting. They are effective only while they are worn, and fertility returns immediately after use. In contrast, sterilization is a permanent method. It involves severing or blocking the vas deferens, the tubes that transport sperm. This prevents sperm from joining with other seminal fluids, so while a man will still ejaculate after sterilization, his ejaculate will not contain sperm. Sterilization and condoms are relatively safe forms of birth control and impact the body in a low-risk way. Researchers are exploring new contraceptives for men, including injections, pills, and fertility immunizations, but none of these methods are ready for consumers.[5]

Female Fertility

Though menstruation is the most noticeable part of a woman's cycle, the main event is ovulation. The first half of a cycle, beginning with menstruation, prepares the body for ovulation. The second half of a cycle responds to ovulation, either by beginning a pregnancy or preparing for menstruation. A brief description of anatomy will help you better understand the processes of ovulation and conception.

External Anatomy

The vulva refers to all the external parts of female genitalia. Unfortunately, many girls believe that their parts "down there" are too dirty, ugly, or secret to observe, touch, and discuss. Knowledge of a woman's own body helps her to protect her health and enjoy sexual intercourse. There is great variety between vulvas in amount of hair, color, fullness of the vaginal lips, and overall size. Using a hand mirror to observe your own body is a good

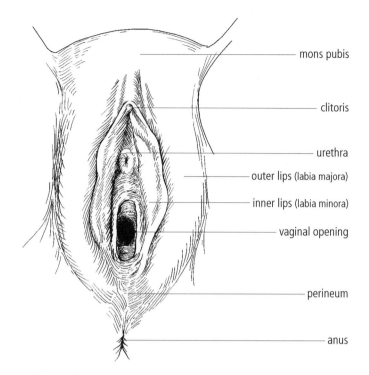

mons pubis

clitoris

urethra

outer lips (labia majora)

inner lips (labia minora)

vaginal opening

perineum

anus

Fig. 3.4. Female External Reproductive Anatomy.

way to begin learning about and appreciating the uniqueness of your body.

Most of the vulva is covered with hair, and the soft, fatty skin beneath the pubic hair is the mons pubis (also called mons veneris), which protects the internal reproductive organs. Below the mons pubis is the top of the vaginal lips. The inner vaginal lips come together to form the hood of the clitoris. This skin protects the clitoris, a small organ that contains many sensitive nerve endings. The clitoris is the female equivalent of a penis, both developing from a similar set of fetal cells. When aroused, the clitoris fills with blood and becomes highly sensitive to pressure or touch. Many women reach orgasm by clitoral stimulation, not by vaginal intercourse.

The rest of the vulva is covered by two sets of lips, the inner and outer vaginal lips. The inner lips are folds of very soft skin. Like the clitoris, the inner lips (also called labia minora) become engorged with blood and darken in color during sexual arousal. The outer lips (also called labia majora) are made of soft skin and often have some hair on the outside. This skin, though soft, is tougher than the inner lips and serves as protection for the entire vulva. Below the clitoris is the urethral meatus, or the opening of the urethra. This opening channels urine from the bladder out of the body.

Below the urethral opening is the vaginal opening, the outer entrance to the vagina, an incredibly elastic and strong four-to six-inch-long passageway between the vulva and cervix. The vagina receives the penis during intercourse and serves as a passageway for the birth of a baby. The tightness of the vagina provides sexual pleasure for both the man and woman, yet the vagina stretches enough to allow a baby to pass through. After childbirth the vagina usually returns to relative tightness. The vagina also produces fluids during sexual arousal that provide lubrication for intercourse. This fluid is different from cervical fluid produced during fertile times, because vaginal fluid does not sustain and extend the life of sperm. The area of skin between the vulva and the rectum is the perineum. This tender tissue is sometimes cut during childbirth to increase space for the baby's passage; this procedure is called an episiotomy.

Most women are born with a hymen, a thin tissue that partially and sometimes totally covers the vaginal opening. Some girls break the hymen by bicycling, gymnastics, or other strenuous activity, while other girls' hymens remain intact until use of tampons or sexual intercourse. Breaking the hymen is sometimes quite painful, but most girls and women break their hymens without noticing it. Sometimes a doctor may stretch the hymen prior to first intercourse if a gynecological exam reveals the hymen is intact and covers much of the vaginal opening.

The external genitalia serve many functions: they excite men by scent and appearance; they facilitate intercourse, childbirth, and menstruation; and they protect the internal reproductive organs. The internal organs prepare the body for ovulation and sustain the body through pregnancies.

Internal Reproductive Anatomy

Most women can feel the upper end of the vagina by reaching a clean finger or two inside the vagina. The cervix is located at the bottom of the uterus (or the upper end of the vagina). It has a small opening (the cervical os) that allows sperm to pass from the vagina into the uterus, cervical fluids to flow down into the vagina, and a baby to exit the uterus. The cervix is lined with many crevices that produce fluid and house sperm as they wait to move up to the fallopian tubes. The os opens slightly when a woman is fertile and closes when she is infertile. It opens very wide during childbirth.

The uterus (also called the womb) is a pear-shaped muscular organ that provides space for a growing fetus. Each month the endometrium (also called the uterine lining) builds up in preparation for a pregnancy. If pregnancy does not occur, the endometrium is shed during menstruation. If pregnancy does occur, the endometrium provides nourishment to the fetus.

The uterus is centered in the body, and fallopian tubes extend from it on both sides. The fallopian tubes transport the egg from ovary to uterus. Fertilization also occurs in the fallopian tubes. The tubes end with fingerlike extensions. At ovulation, the "fingers" move to envelop the ovary, receiving the egg safely for transport through the tubes.

The ovaries are two almond-sized glands that contain up to a million immature eggs. In contrast to men who produce sperm every day, women are born with all the eggs they will ever have. This means the egg that became you was present in your grandmother's womb, in the fetus that became your mother! During each cycle, about fifteen eggs begin to develop, and one eventually becomes dominant and ovulates. Each egg is protected by a follicle that encircles it with fluid. Usually one egg is released each cycle, but sometimes two are released, and if both are fertilized and implanted, twins result.

56

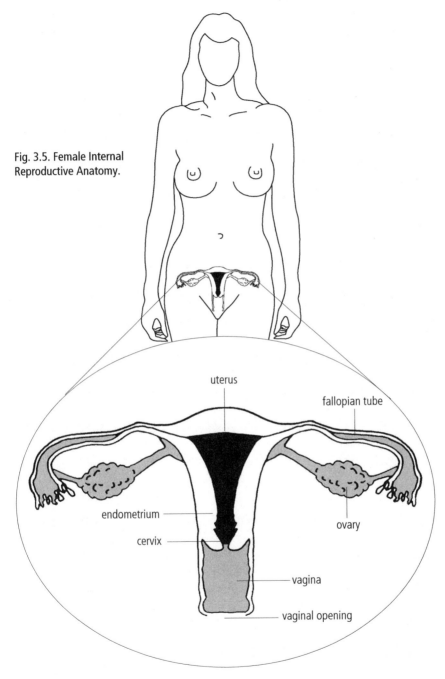

Fig. 3.5. Female Internal Reproductive Anatomy.

The Female Cycle

A woman may desire only a few children, but her ovaries may release more than four hundred eggs during her lifetime. The body prepares for pregnancy every cycle, regardless of whether the woman desires pregnancy. Contraception frustrates this insistent biological process. Understanding the female cycle will allow you to better consider your answer to the question, when does life begin? Your answer to that question can help you exclude some contraceptive methods and consider others.

Pre-ovulation

A cycle begins with menstruation, the shedding of the endometrium that built up during the second half of the previous cycle. Through menstruation and the days following, Follicle Stimulating Hormone (FSH) prompts the initial maturation of ten to fifteen eggs in the ovaries. The follicles that envelop the eggs produce estrogen. One egg becomes dominant, continuing to mature and produce estrogen, while the other eggs disintegrate. When estrogen levels reach a critical level, this triggers another hormone, Luteinizing Hormone (LH), to surge and cause the egg to burst out of the ovary. After ovulation, the egg falls into the pelvic cavity, and the fingerlike extremities of the fallopian tubes pick it up and bring it into the tubes.

Women who experience irregular cycles may look to this stage for explanation. Estrogen is responsive to stress, diet, and other factors, so a woman who experiences a career change, a death, a severe storm, or some other stress may find her cycle is longer that month. Women with extremely low body weight, who take steroids, or who exercise excessively may not menstruate for months or years due to the effects of these conditions on estrogen. Perhaps this is God's way of preventing pregnancy in a woman whose body or whose stress levels may make pregnancy risky.

The primary signs of fertility in the pre-ovulation stage are fertile-quality cervical fluid and changes in the cervix. As estro-

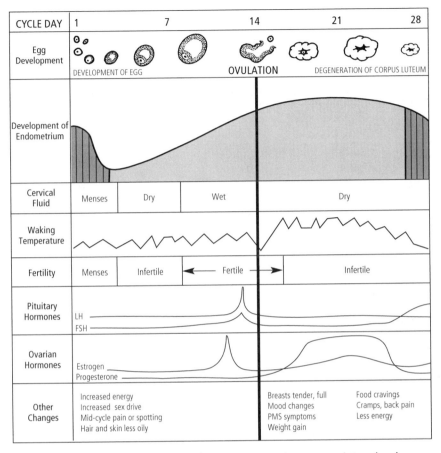

CYCLE DAY	1		7		14		21		28

Fig. 3.6. The Events of the Menstrual Cycle. A woman experiences many internal and external changes associated with her changing hormones.

gen increases, the cervix begins to produce fluid that flows through the vagina, providing sustenance and transport to sperm. Sperm may live for up to five days in this fluid awaiting ovulation. Fertile fluid can be creamy, clear, or opaque, and usually stretches between the fingers like egg white. The cervix changes as well, rising in the vagina, opening, and becoming wet and soft. A helpful acronym for a fertile cervix is SHOW: soft, high, open, wet. Fertility awareness training can enable you to observe these signs accurately.

Secondary signs of fertility in the pre-ovulation stage include clear skin, bright eyes, high energy, and increasing libido (sex drive). Secondary signs are not accurate enough for charting fertility, but many women find it helpful to track changes in appearance, weight, diet, and libido over the course of their cycles. Most women feel stronger, healthier, and more attractive in the pre-ovulation stage.

Ovulation: The Main Event

Ovulation occurs when the egg literally bursts through the wall of the ovary, prompted by the surge of luteinizing hormone. For many women, ovulation occurs around twelve to fifteen days after the first day of menstruation, but this varies for different women. The egg usually lives for twelve to twenty-four hours. If it is not fertilized in that time, it deteriorates. Sometimes two eggs are released together, and in even more rare circumstances, two eggs are released twelve to twenty-four hours apart, potentially resulting in twins.

Many women do not experience signs of ovulation. Some women report pain on their right or left side at the time of ovulation. Others report midcycle bleeding, which can be a sign of ovulation. Ovulation is also indicated by a rise in waking temperature and a drying of cervical fluid.

Post-ovulation Phase

Following the release of the egg, the follicle that held the egg deteriorates. The follicle, called the corpus luteum, remains in the ovary and starts releasing progesterone. If pregnancy does not occur, the corpus luteum deteriorates, progesterone levels fall, and menstruation occurs. The post-ovulation phase is very consistent between cycles, lasting between twelve to sixteen days for different women. If a woman has irregular cycles, it is often due to fluctuations in the pre-ovulatory phase. Once ovulation occurs, the body is influenced by progesterone, which is not very responsive to stress. Perhaps this is God's way of maintaining an early pregnancy, regardless of a woman's stress levels or life changes. Once pregnancy occurs, progesterone takes over and sustains the new life.

Primary signs of the post-ovulation phase include a raised waking temperature, scant or dry cervical fluid, and a lowered, hardened, closed cervix. Secondary signs of the post-ovulation phase often include premenstrual symptoms: blemished complexion, dull hair, constipation, irritability, moodiness, weight gain, water retention, and food cravings. Scientists are not entirely sure whether the body is responding to high levels of progesterone, low levels of estrogen, or something else. One Catholic scientist suggests the body is mourning the loss of potential pregnancy; a woman may become depressed or irritable when she discovers "she is about to lose the home she was building for a baby."[6]

Conception: The Result of Combined Fertility

Remember what is necessary for conception: sperm + egg + fertile cervical fluid. Conception is the result of combined fertility. Men produce sperm every day and are fertile with each act of intercourse. Women, on the other hand, only produce fertile cervical fluid and an egg some of the time. The egg's lifespan is just twelve to twenty-four hours, yet a woman's fertile period can last up to eight to ten days. This is because cervical fluid sustains sperm for days before and after ovulation. Therefore, a couple is in a state of combined fertility for approximately one-third of each cycle.

Once inside the vagina, sperm encounter one of two conditions: hostility or friendliness. Most of the time the vagina is an acidic environment, hostile to sperm. In addition, the cervix is closed, creating a locked door for sperm attempting to enter the uterus. Sperm face a hostile hallway with a closed door at the end and die within several hours. When a woman is fertile, however, her vaginal environment is friendly. The cervix opens, making way for the sperm to swim up to the fallopian tubes. The hallway, or the vagina itself, is coated with fluids that flow down from the cervix. These fluids are glucose-rich and have a ladderlike

MALE FERTILITY

Men are fertile 100% of the time

FEMALE FERTILITY

Menses	Dry	Wet Cervical Fluid	Dry

Women are fertile 30 percent of the time, when fertile cervical fluid is present (and a few days following).

COMBINED FERTILITY

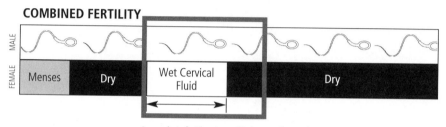

A couple is fertile about 10 days each month.

Fig. 3.7. Combined Fertility. Men are fertile all the time, and women are fertile around one-third of the time. It takes combined fertility for pregnancy to occur.

microscopic structure that allows sperm to swim speedily up to the fallopian tubes.

Sperm may wait in the crevices of the cervix for up to five days awaiting ovulation. This means that while you had sex on Monday, conception may happen on Friday! Sperm must swim through the uterus and into the fallopian tubes to meet the egg. When fertilization occurs, it is usually in the outer third of the fallopian tubes. The cilia, small hairlike projections in the fallopian tubes, move the fertilized egg along and deposit it in the uterus. The fertilized egg then burrows into the uterine lining and pregnancy begins.

The fertilized and implanted egg immediately begins releasing a pregnancy hormone, Human Chorionic Gonadotropin

(HCG, the hormone measured by home pregnancy tests). HCG communicates with the corpus luteum, telling it to stay alive and continue producing progesterone beyond its usual lifespan. After several months, the placenta takes over the work of the corpus luteum, sustaining the endometrium and nourishing the fetus.

Early signs of pregnancy may include breast and nipple tenderness, fatigue, nausea, or light bleeding. Some women experience these symptoms as soon as one week after fertilization. Home pregnancy tests that measure HCG levels are accurate, but sometimes women get false negative results because they take the test before HCG levels are high enough to be measured by the test. Charting cycles with fertility awareness is another way of identifying early pregnancy.

How Birth Control Intervenes in Female Fertility

Contraceptives influence a woman's body in various ways. Contraceptive research and development have focused more on women than men, so women have more contraceptive options. They also face greater medical risk, however, because many female contraceptives impact the body more dramatically than do male methods. Female contraceptives are grouped in several categories according to the way they work. I will explain how contraceptives in each category work (the mechanism of action) and give examples of the methods, but if you're unfamiliar with the examples, don't worry. Each method will be discussed in detail later in the book.

Behavioral Methods

With behavioral methods a couple makes behavioral choices to prevent sperm and egg from meeting, though each method accomplishes this purpose in different ways. Behavioral methods do not affect the body and are immediately reversible. These methods include self-observation methods, the Standard Days Method, withdrawal, and the lactational amenorrhea method.

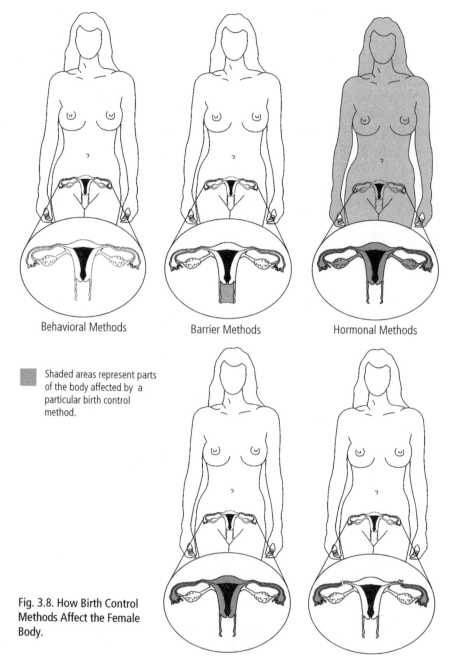

Behavioral Methods

Barrier Methods

Hormonal Methods

Shaded areas represent parts of the body affected by a particular birth control method.

Fig. 3.8. How Birth Control Methods Affect the Female Body.

Intrauterine Devices

Permanent Methods

Barrier Methods

The mechanism of action for barrier methods is to prevent conception by preventing sperm from entering the uterus. Barrier methods affect the female genitals while they are being used, and their effects are immediately reversible. Barrier methods for women include the female condom, diaphragm, contraceptive sponge, and cervical cap. All of these are most effectively used in combination with a spermicide.

Hormonal Methods

Hormonal methods affect the entire body because they act on the brain, changing the way the brain sends hormonal messages to the reproductive system. Their mechanism of action is complex and varies across the different types of methods. In general, these methods prevent pregnancy by preventing ovulation. Second, they change the quality of cervical fluid, making it more difficult for sperm to swim. Third, they change the quality of the endometrium. It is possible for a woman to ovulate while using hormonal methods, and if she does, the fertilized egg may be unable to implant in the endometrium. Hormonal methods are reversible when use is discontinued. Examples of these methods include combined hormonal contraceptives, progestin-only methods, and emergency contraception. These hormones are packaged in many ways, including pills, implants, injections, the intrauterine system, the patch, and the vaginal ring.

Intrauterine Devices (IUDs)

The mechanism of action for intrauterine devices is not entirely understood, but they seem to work in three ways. First, the IUD immobilizes sperm, making them unable to swim through the uterus to the fallopian tubes. Second, it speeds the transport of the ovum through the fallopian tubes, shortening the time available for conception. Third, the IUD affects the quality of the endometrium, though the impact of this effect on conception or implantation is not entirely clear. The IUD is a reversible form of birth control. It is a medical device, usually shaped like a T, placed inside the uterus. Conventional IUDs do not carry hormones, but new IUDs (sometimes called Intrauterine Systems or IUSs) do.

Sterilization

Female sterilization affects the fallopian tubes. It prevents pregnancy by preventing the sperm and egg from meeting. It accomplishes this by tying, clipping, or otherwise blocking the fallopian tubes. It affects only the fallopian tubes and is not reversible.

Questions for Conversation

Consider ways in which contraception intervenes in your life, your body, and the life that may result from sexual intercourse. You may find that some interventions are too invasive, or too late in the process of life, to be considered.

1. How do you feel about the reproductive parts of your body? What adjectives would you use to describe them? Do you think your attitudes are, or will be, beneficial to your marriage?
2. By considering how contraception affects the body, would you rule out any contraceptives as possibilities for you? Which methods would you strongly consider?
3. By considering how contraception intervenes in the process of life, would you rule out any methods? Which methods would you strongly consider?
4. At this point, what methods seem like the best possibilities for you? What else do you want to know about them before making a decision?

4

Don't Try This at Home

Notoriously Ineffective Methods

Masturbation will make you go blind or grow hair on the palms of your hands. If your boyfriend is aroused and you refuse to have sex, his testicles will develop a disease. Sexual ability varies by race. People with sexual experience make the best lovers. Premarital sex is less of a sin if you do it with your fiancé(e) than with a boyfriend or girlfriend. Young, beautiful, thin people have the best sex. Not true! Sexual myths are like the childhood game of telephone. They're whispered and repeated among friends, often increasing in extravagance and inaccuracy with each telling.

Junior high and high school students are known to believe and spread sexual myths, much to the chagrin of health teachers and parents. Teenagers, however, are not the only ones with confused and bizarre beliefs about sex. Adults hold mistaken beliefs as well, and when these myths are about contraception, the results can be costly.

In this chapter we'll look at the most common contraceptive myths, though we won't cover all of them. Creative contraceptive inventions are spread by word of mouth, and it is difficult to keep up with people's creativity. If you hear about a way to avoid pregnancy that sounds too good to be true, it probably is. Consult reference books or ask a medical provider before experimenting with contraceptives. Understanding how fertility works is your best weapon against contraceptive myths. Most of these myths can be debunked simply by reviewing the processes of fertility and conception discussed in the last chapter.

Abstinence in Marriage

One myth is that abstinence within marriage is a good form of birth control. Abstinence is, in fact, the only birth control method with 100 percent effectiveness, but it is not a good idea for married couples. Some self-observation methods include brief periods of abstinence, but if abstinence is a couple's only form of birth control, it is likely to do more harm than good. Because sexual intercourse is an important aspect of marriage, long-term abstinence can lead to emotional distance, physical frustration, and separateness.

Abstinence *outside* of marriage, however, is a great birth control method. Choosing abstinence as a way of preventing pregnancy shows forethought and decisiveness about sexual boundaries.

Avoiding Female Orgasm

Some people believe a woman becomes pregnant only if she experiences orgasm. This myth apparently stems from the biology of rabbits. Female rabbits are "reactor ovulators," that is, they ovulate in response to copulation. Over time and through many tellings, this biological fact was misconstrued as a story about women's orgasm.

The cervix opens and produces fluid that transports and sustains sperm on their journey to the fallopian tubes. Changes in the cervix and ovulation are triggered by hormonal changes, not by sexual intercourse or orgasm. Sperm movement, ovulation, and fertilization happen independently of orgasm. This myth makes sex less fun for women, so don't believe it!

Denying That You Are Having Sex

Self-delusion is perhaps the most powerful kind of lie. Christians are especially vulnerable to this because they believe unmarried sex is sinful. Vicki, a nineteen-year-old single woman, said to me, "I didn't plan to have a sexual relationship. It just sort of happened. We were together a lot, we were kissing, and then sex just sort of happened." Some say their relationship isn't really sexual because they have sex only occasionally. Sexual partners may lie to each other and to themselves, silently pretending that although sex happened once or twice, it surely won't happen again. Planning, purchasing, and using birth control shows forethought and intent, and sin that was planned in advance seems worse than sin that is spontaneous. Not true! Be honest with yourself! If you are in a relationship in which sex has ever happened, even once, be honest about it. Avoiding pregnancy is just one part of this issue, but it is an important aspect that, if neglected, can result in pregnancy.

Douching after Sex

Rinsing the vagina with water or acidic fluids after sex has been a long-standing contraceptive practice in many cultures. One account of contraceptive use in nineteenth-century America describes a woman breaking the ice that had formed on her basin of water during the night in order to rinse her vagina after sex. Douching is more effective than using no contraception at all, but it is not as effective as modern methods. It should not be relied upon for pregnancy avoidance. A related myth is that acidic fluids such as pickle juice, Mountain Dew, or Pepsi kill sperm. Researchers have found that some acidic fluids kill sperm in a test tube but only in laboratory conditions. A person cannot achieve acid levels sufficient to kill all sperm in the vagina. Also, sperm swim into the cervix within seconds of ejaculation, which is the biological fact that renders this method a myth.

Douching has been discredited as a contraceptive method for many decades. In 1940, for example, medical doctor Philip Williams stated that douching was one of the most prevalent contraceptive practices at that time. Women were douching incorrectly, without adequate pressure, and were concocting acidic solutions that were poisonous. He concluded, "The high percentage of failures following the use of the douche as a contraceptive measure discards it from any serious consideration."[1] More than half a century later, however, this myth persists.

Herbs

The use of herbs for contraception and abortion has been pervasive throughout history and world cultures.[2] Herbs can interfere with ovulation, the quality of cervical fluid, sperm viability, implantation, and endometrial quality. Contraceptive herbs include Queen Anne's Lace (wild carrot seed), wild yam, neem, pomegranate, rutin, tansy, cotton root bark, and many others. Today, women attracted to herbs are often those who have had negative experiences with conventional contraception or who value natural, nonmedical treatments. Some natural health practitioners offer herbal remedies for contraception, and websites sell herbs for birth control and at-home abortions.

Herbal contraceptives can be effective, but they also can be extremely dangerous. Unfortunately, corporations and foundations that fund research on pharmaceutical contraceptives rarely fund research on herbal contraceptives, so knowledge about these methods tends to be anecdotal. Because herbs are not regulated by the FDA, their potency and purity varies from batch to batch. In addition, quantities of herbs needed for contraception are unknown. One website advises taking quantities that "feel right to you."[3] This website also acknowledges that most herbalists discourage women from using herbs as contraceptives due to the dangers associated with herbal contraceptives. Herbal contraceptives are so dangerous that they may harm your body, and if you do become pregnant, they may have caused permanent and severe damage to the fetus. Because of their known effectiveness in other cultures, herbal contraceptives may become a more viable option in the future, but at present they should be avoided.

Homemade Spermicides

Historically, people have made spermicides from crocodile dung, lemon, and other acids. Today, people sometimes make their own from household disinfectants, cosmetic products, or food. While various acidic substances may have some spermicidal properties, their effectiveness is unpredictable, and they may cause serious harm to the user. Use only medically approved spermicides. In the United States, Nonoxynol 9, or N-9, is the most readily available, safe spermicide. It is available on condoms, in vaginal suppositories, and in spermicidal lubricants, foams, jellies, and creams.

Improvised Condoms

Condoms seem fairly simple. Why not improvise and make one out of plastic wrap, a plastic bag, or a surgical glove? Historically, condoms have been a product of creative inspiration, fashioned from silk, fabric, leather, or animal intestines. These condoms were also washed and reused, which is not recommended. Since the development of vulcanized rubber in the mid–nineteenth century, condoms have improved in quality, sensation, and effectiveness. Never make your own condom. It could break, carry infectious bacteria, or be painful during sex. Purchase condoms and use them according to directions printed on the box.

Intuition

Some women feel confident that they can sense when they are fertile. This is a myth. Women experience primary and secondary signs of fertility, including ovulatory pain, increased cervical fluid, increased sex drive, clear complexion, increased energy, and other symptoms. These sensations do not, however, provide accurate guides for timing intercourse. Women can learn to be aware of their fertility, but they should do so only from a qualified instructor. Women's intuition is a powerful thing, but it cannot account for variations in cycles from month to month or the extended life of sperm within the cervix.

Standing Up during Intercourse

Another myth is that pregnancy can't occur if you have sex standing up or in some unusual position. Ovulation and sperm movement do not respond to sexual position.

Prayer

Prayer is perhaps the most common emergency contraceptive used by Christians, both married and not. Unfortunately, the Lord seems unwilling to be used as a contraceptive. Prayer is a wonderful thing, but it is a sign of irresponsibility, not spirituality, to rely on it to prevent pregnancy.

Urinating or Bathing after Sex

This myth is similar to the myth about douching. It says urinating, showering, or bathing after sex can expel sperm from the vagina. Because sperm are so speedy, they swim into the cervix within seconds of ejaculation, making urination or bathing an ineffective contraceptive. Urinating or bathing after sex will expel some sperm from the vagina, but this will not reliably prevent pregnancy.

Will Power

Some people believe a woman won't get pregnant unless she wants to. As infertile couples know, wishing, hoping, and willing sperm and egg to come together just doesn't work. Likewise, will power will not prevent a pregnancy. Like prayer, it is a strategy that people will likely employ anyway, but it should not be relied upon as an effective contraceptive.

Part 2

Behavioral Methods

5

Self-Observation
Methods

Fertility Awareness Method
and Natural Family Planning

S elf-observation methods enable a woman to observe her body's signs of fertility on a daily basis. With this method she observes, records, and interprets her cervical fluid, temperature, and cervix position (though it isn't always necessary to monitor all three of these signs). She uses this information to make choices about intercourse. To avoid pregnancy, she may abstain from intercourse or use a barrier method when she is fertile.

Mechanism of Action

Self-observation methods allow a couple to avoid pregnancy by making choices about intercourse based upon the woman's

fertility. The woman daily observes and charts her fertility symptoms and interprets them according to a set of rules. On days when
she is fertile, the couple abstains or uses a barrier method to prevent pregnancy. On days when she is infertile, the couple may
have sex without any contraception. The woman records her fertility symptoms on a chart (see sample chart, fig. 5.1).

A woman's body responds to hormones in many ways, as
described in chapter 3. Many of these symptoms are noticeable,
but only a few are reliable enough to use for fertility awareness.
The three symptoms used in self-observation methods are cervical fluid, waking temperature, and cervix position.[1] The most
important of these are cervical fluid and waking temperature.[2]

Learning to observe and interpret cervical fluid is the first step
in learning self-observation methods. After menstruation, cervical fluid changes from dry to wet and back to dry in the course
of a menstrual cycle. Many women notice more vaginal discharge
or a feeling of wetness during their cycle. The first half of a
woman's cycle, from the beginning of menstruation to ovulation,
is estrogen-dominant. Estrogen levels rise, stimulated by the
growing egg inside the ovary. As estrogen rises, cervical fluid
becomes increasingly plentiful, slippery, and stretchy. Sometimes
a woman may stretch this fluid between her fingers to five or even
ten inches! This fluid provides nourishment and transport to
sperm, allowing them to live for several days inside the cervix
and to swim toward the fallopian tubes. When a woman is producing fertile-quality cervical fluid, she is fertile. When cervical
fluid is absent (the vagina is "dry" like the inside of the cheek),
she is infertile.

To observe this sign, a woman uses her finger or a tissue to
wipe across the vaginal opening. She checks for fluid several
times a day—checking before using the bathroom is a convenient way to make it a habit. She looks at the fluid and tests it for
stretchiness between two fingers.

The second indicator is a rise in waking temperature (also
called basal body temperature). Near midcycle, hormones stimulate ovulation; the egg bursts from its follicle and travels into
the fallopian tube. The egg's follicle is left behind at the ovary,

becoming the corpus luteum. The corpus luteum produces progesterone, which causes a rise in temperature that is sustained throughout the second half of a cycle, from ovulation to menstruation. To observe this sign, a woman takes her temperature daily upon waking, before eating, drinking, or walking. When she discerns a temperature rise according to a set of rules, she knows she has ovulated and her fertile time will end a few days later.

There are two commonly used self-observation methods: the sympto-thermal method and the ovulation method. The sympto-thermal method uses both cervical fluid and waking temperature to determine the fertile time. Cervix changes are an optional indicator. The ovulation method (also called the Billings Method) relies on cervical fluid alone.

There is a third method, which is rarely used. It's the basal body temperature method (BBT). It relies on temperature alone and requires a much longer time of abstinence or barrier use, allowing unprotected intercourse only after ovulation.

Fertility monitoring systems are being developed, and some are available on-line. They are not yet approved by the FDA, nor are they on the market in the United States. Home fertility monitors are small, hand-held computers that read hormone levels, telling a woman whether or not she is fertile on a given day. Some measure hormones in urine, and others use saliva. These technologies have been used primarily to treat infertility, but they are becoming available for pregnancy prevention as well.[3] These computerized systems do not necessarily provide more accurate information than standard self-observation methods.

Types of Self-Observation Approaches

There are two main approaches to self-observation methods of birth control. Natural family planning (NFP) and the fertility awareness method (FAM) use the same scientific understandings of fertility and the same methods for charting and interpreting fertility signs. People who use NFP or FAM may use the sympto-thermal method, ovulation method, or basal body tem-

Cycle Day	Date	Intercourse	Cervical Fluid Description	Fertile Days	Waking Temperature	Cycle Day
1	1/9		menses		97 1 2 3 4 5 6 ● 8 9 98 1 2 3 4 5 6 7 8 9 99	1
2	1/10		menses		97 1 2 3 4 5 ● 7 8 9 98 1 2 3 4 5 6 7 8 9 99	2
3	1/11		menses		97 1 2 3 4 ● 6 7 8 9 98 1 2 3 4 5 6 7 8 9 99	3
4	1/12		menses		97 1 2 3 4 ● 6 7 8 9 98 1 2 3 4 5 6 7 8 9 99	4
5	1/13	*	spotting, dry		97 1 2 3 4 5 6 ● 8 9 98 1 2 3 4 5 6 7 8 9 99	5
6	1/14		dry		97 1 2 3 4 ● 6 7 8 9 98 1 2 3 4 5 6 7 8 9 99	6
7	1/15	*	dry		97 1 2 3 4 5 ● 7 8 9 98 1 2 3 4 5 6 7 8 9 99	7
8	1/16		dry		97 1 2 3 ● 5 6 7 8 9 98 1 2 3 4 5 6 7 8 9 99	8
9	1/17		creamy, wet		97 1 2 3 4 ● 6 7 8 9 98 1 2 3 4 5 6 7 8 9 99	9
10	1/18		wet, creamy		97 1 2 3 4 ● 6 7 8 9 98 1 2 3 4 5 6 7 8 9 99	10
11	1/19		stretchy		97 1 2 3 4 5 ● 7 8 9 98 1 2 3 4 5 6 7 8 9 99	11
12	1/20		stretchy, "egg-white"		97 1 2 3 4 5 6 7 ● 9 98 1 2 3 4 5 6 7 8 9 99	12
13	1/21		wet, stretchy		97 1 2 3 4 5 6 7 ● 9 98 1 2 3 4 5 6 7 8 9 99	13
14	1/22		wet, stretchy		97 1 2 3 4 5 ● 7 8 9 98 1 2 3 4 5 6 7 8 9 99	14
15	1/23		wet, stretchy		97 1 2 3 4 5 6 ● 8 9 98 1 2 3 4 5 6 7 8 9 99	15
16	1/24		dry		97 1 2 3 4 5 6 7 8 9 98 1 2 3 ● 5 6 7 8 9 99	16
17	1/25		dry		97 1 2 3 4 5 6 7 8 9 98 1 2 3 4 ● 6 7 8 9 99	17
18	1/26		dry		97 1 2 3 4 5 6 7 8 9 98 1 2 3 4 ● 6 7 8 9 99	18
19	1/27		dry		97 1 2 3 4 5 6 7 8 9 98 1 ● 3 4 5 6 7 8 9 99	19
20	1/28	*	dry		97 1 2 3 4 5 6 7 8 9 98 1 2 ● 4 5 6 7 8 9 99	20
21	1/29		dry		97 1 2 3 4 5 6 7 8 9 98 1 2 3 ● 5 6 7 8 9 99	21
22	1/30		dry		97 1 2 3 4 5 6 7 8 9 98 1 2 3 4 ● 6 7 8 9 99	22
23	1/31		dry		97 1 2 3 4 5 6 7 8 9 98 ● 2 3 4 5 6 7 8 9 99	23
24	2/1	*	dry		97 1 2 3 4 5 6 7 8 9 98 1 ● 3 4 5 6 7 8 9 99	24
25	2/2	*	dry		97 1 2 3 4 5 6 7 8 9 98 1 2 ● 4 5 6 7 8 9 99	25
26	2/3		dry		97 1 2 3 4 5 6 7 8 9 98 1 2 ● 4 5 6 7 8 9 99	26
27	2/4		dry		97 1 2 3 4 5 6 7 8 9 98 1 2 ● 4 5 6 7 8 9 99	27
28	2/5	*	dry		97 1 2 3 4 5 6 7 8 9 98 ● 2 3 4 5 6 7 8 9 99	28
29	2/6		menses		97 1 2 3 4 5 6 ● 8 9 98 1 2 3 4 5 6 7 8 9 99	29
30	2/7				97 1 2 3 4 5 6 7 8 9 98 1 2 3 4 5 6 7 8 9 99	30
31	2/8				97 1 2 3 4 5 6 7 8 9 98 1 2 3 4 5 6 7 8 9 99	31
32					97 1 2 3 4 5 6 7 8 9 98 1 2 3 4 5 6 7 8 9 99	32
33					97 1 2 3 4 5 6 7 8 9 98 1 2 3 4 5 6 7 8 9 99	33
34					97 1 2 3 4 5 6 7 8 9 98 1 2 3 4 5 6 7 8 9 99	34
35					97 1 2 3 4 5 6 7 8 9 98 1 2 3 4 5 6 7 8 9 99	35
36					97 1 2 3 4 5 6 7 8 9 98 1 2 3 4 5 6 7 8 9 99	36
37					97 1 2 3 4 5 6 7 8 9 98 1 2 3 4 5 6 7 8 9 99	37
38					97 1 2 3 4 5 6 7 8 9 98 1 2 3 4 5 6 7 8 9 99	38

Fig. 5.1. Sample Self-Observation Chart. After her period, this woman's cervical fluid is dry, then wet and stretchy, and then dry again after ovulation. Her temperature rises on day 16 in response to ovulation.

perature. The difference between the two approaches is in their views on abstinence.

Natural family planning (NFP) requires the use of abstinence during fertile times. This is the method approved by the Roman Catholic Church and some other religious groups that forbid contraception. If you tell someone you are using natural family planning, you are saying you chart your fertility and abstain during fertile times. NFP instructors refer to this method as child spacing, not birth control. It is a part of married life that allows couples to make wise choices about when to reproduce.

The fertility awareness method (FAM) allows women or couples to use barrier methods during fertile times, though abstinence may also be used. It is up to the couple to decide what is best for them. If you tell someone you are using fertility awareness, you are saying you chart your fertility and may or may not use barrier methods during fertile times. FAM is not associated with any religion and does not take a stance on the morality of contraception. It is used by Christians, women who value natural health care, and women who cannot use other methods for medical reasons.

It is important to understand these approaches when seeking an instructor or talking with others who use self-observation methods. Students in NFP courses will hear an anticontraception morality along with knowledge of fertility. Students in FAM courses will not necessarily hear any Christian morality associated with the method. In either course, a couple may discuss together or with trusted advisors the theological and spiritual implications of what they are learning.

People often refer to these methods inaccurately. Sometimes people "intuit" fertility or use no method at all but say they are using NFP or FAM. Sometimes people claim to be using fertility awareness but have not been properly trained. It's no wonder why the classic joke is still in circulation: "What do you call a couple who uses natural family planning? Parents!" People also refer to the calendar method (also called the rhythm method), which is no longer taught by the Catholic Church and has effectiveness rates much lower than NFP and FAM.[4]

Effectiveness

With correct use of self-observation methods, about one to three out of a hundred women will become pregnant in one year

81

of use. When you add people who sometimes use the method incorrectly, about twenty out of a hundred will become pregnant in one year.[5]

A sizable proportion of unintended pregnancies are due to improper teaching and use of the method.[6] Some couples create their own self-observation methods based on intuition or inconsistent charting. Some couples use self-observation methods after reading a book or website without taking a course from a trained instructor. Optimum effectiveness rates are attainable only when a couple learns a scientifically based self-observation method from a trained instructor and then practices the method consistently and correctly.

There are slight variations between the effectiveness rates of the ovulation method, sympto-thermal method, and basal body temperature method, but all are over 97 percent effective when used correctly. In addition, there is no significant difference in pregnancy rates between couples who use barriers during the fertile time and couples who abstain.[7]

How to Maximize Effectiveness

Learn the method properly. Self-observation methods are best learned in a class that meets several times. This gives you opportunities to ask questions, learn the method as you observe several cycles, and receive feedback from an instructor's review of your charts. Self-observation methods should not be learned solely from a book. It takes two to three months to learn to observe and interpret your fertility patterns accurately.

Find a trained instructor. Natural family planning instructors may be accessed on-line or by inquiring at a local Catholic church. Organizations offering natural family planning courses include The Couple to Couple League (www.ccli.org), Billings Ovulation Method Association–U.S.A. (www.familyplanning.net), Georgetown University's Institute for Reproductive Health (www.irh.org), and the Family of the Americas Foundation (www.woomb.org). Fertility awareness instructors are more difficult to find, but you can begin by asking at women's health clinics, health food co-ops, or natural health-care clinics. Numerous published resources may also help you get started. Two excellent books include *Taking Charge of Your Fertility* and *Your Fertility Signs.*[8]

Use self-observation consistently. Self-observation methods must be used daily to be effective. If you forget to check cervical fluid or temperature on a given day, consider that day fertile! Never assume that you are fertile or infertile based on past cycles.

Advantages

Minimal daily observation and record keeping. After an initial period of learning, a woman spends one to two minutes per day observing and recording her fertility signs.

Natural. Self-observation methods do not affect the body in any way. They are low-tech, noninvasive, and carry no risk of side effects.

Reversible. Fertility is not affected by self-observation methods, so a couple may reverse the method and seek pregnancy at any time.

Allows couples to share the responsibility for contraception. Self-observation methods involve negotiation and communication between spouses as they decide how to respond to a woman's fertility each day. In addition, the man may be involved in recording and interpreting fertility signs.

Does not interrupt intercourse. A woman knows whether or not she is fertile before sexual intimacy begins, so she knows whether or not to use a barrier method at the time of intercourse.

Promotes creative abstinence. During periods of abstinence, which means no contact between penis and vagina, couples develop different ways of expressing sexual intimacy, including verbal expressions of love, hugs and kisses, oral sex, and touch.[9]

Provides other benefits. Self-observation methods provide a woman with extensive information about her reproductive health, which she may use to achieve pregnancy, detect pregnancy, detect impaired fertility, relieve premenstrual symptoms, and detect infection or disease.[10] Many women and men also report greater respect for women and a sense of appreciation about God, the human body, and the process of reproduction.

Does not harm the fetus. If a woman becomes pregnant during or after use of self-observation methods, this will not harm a fetus or infant.

Disadvantages

Requires daily attention. Self-observation methods require daily attention to and charting of fertility signs. Some women find this to be a disadvantage.

May be more complex for certain women. Recent discontinuation of hormonal contraception, recent onset of menstruation, approaching menopause, recent childbirth, or current breast feeding may make self-observation slightly more difficult because these conditions usually cause irregular cycles. However, with extra care a woman can still use self-observation methods effectively under any of these conditions.

Requires cooperation of partner. Like other behavioral methods, self-observation methods require communication and cooperation between spouses.

Requires time and energy. Self-observation methods take the time and energy necessary to learn the method. Most women are able to use the method confidently after two to three months. Many instructional programs involve three to four sessions spread over several months, though some approaches are much more extensive.[11]

Cost

Copies of blank charts and a thermometer may cost approximately ten dollars in the first year of use. Fertility awareness courses are sometimes free but sometimes involve fees ranging from seventy-five to two hundred dollars. If barrier methods such as condoms, spermicides, a cervical cap, or a diaphragm are used during fertile times, these add to the overall cost.

Questions for Conversation

1. What for you is most appealing about self-observation methods? How does your spouse view this method's advantages?

2. What for you is self-observation's most important drawback? How does your spouse view the disadvantages? Are the disadvantages of self-observation methods acceptable to you?

3. Natural family planning (NFP) and fertility awareness method (FAM) approach self-observation methods from different ethical perspectives. Which approach is more consistent with your values?

4. Self-observation methods require daily attention to fertility symptoms and charting. Is this a routine that suits you?

5. How might you express sexual intimacy during fertile times? Would you use a barrier method or abstain? If you would abstain, how might you express love during these times?

6. Will this method allow you to better express and enjoy sexual intimacy? Might it suppress sexual intimacy? Why?

7. Self-observation methods require cooperation between spouses. How might communication and cooperation work out in your relationship? How might you approach potential difficulties?

8. On a scale of one to ten (one meaning "absolutely not" and ten meaning "this looks really good"), how do you rank this method? How does your spouse rank it?

9. As a couple, do you assess self-observation methods in a similar way or in different ways? Are any of your disagreements significant enough to warrant consideration of a different method?

Standard Days Method

T he standard days method (SDM) provides a woman with a clear indicator of her fertile and infertile times. It identifies a fixed number of days during each menstrual cycle when a woman is potentially fertile. To avoid pregnancy, she may abstain from intercourse or use a barrier method during her fertile time.

COURTESY OF THE INSTITUTE FOR REPRODUCTIVE HEALTH, GEORGETOWN UNIVERSITY

Fig. 6.1. To use the standard days method, a woman may use CycleBeads, which indicate her fertile times. She begins by moving the rubber ring to the first bead on the first day of her cycle. She continues to move it one bead per day and is fertile when the rubber ring is on a white bead.

Mechanism of Action

SDM involves abstaining from intercourse or using a barrier on days eight to nineteen of a woman's cycle (the first day of menstruation is day 1).[1] Most women use SDM with the help of CycleBeads, a color-coded string of beads, with each bead representing one day in the menstrual cycle (see fig. 6.1).[2] On the first day of menstrual

87

bleeding, a woman moves the rubber ring to the red bead. Each day she moves the ring to the next bead, following the direction of the arrow. As long as she is on a brown bead, she considers herself not fertile. Any day she is on a white bead, she considers herself fertile. When her period returns, she moves the ring to the red bead and starts again.

A woman may also use the SDM by tracking her cycles without the help of CycleBeads.[3] She may learn the method and use a calendar or other device to count days.

The SDM is designed only for women with most cycles between twenty-six and thirty-two days. Women with longer or shorter cycles will have fertile times that differ from the SDM days. Women whose cycles vary from twenty-six to thirty-two days more than twice a year should use a different method. An instructor or the SDM website (www.cyclebeads.com) can help you determine whether or not your cycles are between twenty-six to thirty-two days.

This method was recently developed by the Institute for Reproductive Health at Georgetown University.[4] It is based upon the scientific knowledge used for self-observation methods but eliminates the need for extensive fertility awareness training.

Effectiveness

With correct use, about five out of a hundred women will become pregnant in one year of use. When you add people who sometimes use the method incorrectly ("typical use"), about twelve out of a hundred women will become pregnant in one year.[5]

When the standard days method fails for a person using it correctly, it is because a woman was fertile on a day that CycleBeads or another standard days system indicated she was infertile and she had unprotected intercourse. This may happen if a woman's cycle is less than twenty-six days or greater than thirty-two days. Even women who normally have regular cycles will occasionally have an unusually short or long cycle. These are the times when the standard days method can fail.

How to Maximize Effectiveness

Be sure this method is appropriate for you. Most of your cycles must be between twenty-six and thirty-two days for this method to be effective. If your cycles are outside this range, you should choose a different method.

Learn the method properly. A woman may learn the SDM in a ten- to fifteen-minute instructional period. The CycleBeads website provides extensive educational material and may help you find an instructor in your area.

Use SDM consistently. CycleBeads must be used daily to be effective, and the fertile days must be observed with abstinence or other contraception. If you forget to use the beads for several days or forget where you are in your cycle, use another method of contraception until your next cycle begins.

Take good care of your supplies. Keep your CycleBeads or standard days method information in a safe place.

Advantages

Natural. The standard days method does not involve hormones or devices that affect the body. It is low-tech, noninvasive, and has no risk of side effects.

Simple and convenient. Using CycleBeads involves a one-time purchase of beads and information, with no required ongoing expense. After an initial period of learning the method, it takes little time or effort on a daily basis.

Easily reversible. Fertility is not affected by the SDM, so a couple may reverse the method and seek pregnancy at any time.

Not used at the time of intercourse. A couple knows whether or not the day is fertile before the time of intercourse and can plan accordingly.

Promotes creative abstinence. Some couples benefit from periods of abstinence (no contact between penis and vagina). While the SDM does not require abstinence, those who choose to abstain may find other ways of expressing sexual intimacy.

Provides other benefits. The SDM may be used "in reverse," using the fertile days to time intercourse for pregnancy achievement.

Does not harm the fetus. If a woman becomes pregnant during or after use of the SDM, it will not harm the fetus or infant.

Disadvantages

May be unreliable for women whose cycles are irregular. Conditions that may cause cycle irregularities include recent discontinuation of hormonal contraception, recent onset of menstruation, approaching menopause, recent childbirth, or current breast-feeding.

Requires cooperation between partners. Like other behavioral methods, the SDM requires communication and cooperation between spouses.

Requires daily attention. A woman must pay attention to her cycle on a daily basis.

Assumes a lengthy period of fertility. The SDM requires a woman to assume she is fertile for twelve days each cycle. Her actual fertility is more likely six to seven days, but this method does not teach her to detect her fertile days. If a woman wants fewer days of abstinence or contraception, she may use a self-observation method such as natural family planning or the fertility awareness method.

Cost

Information about the standard days method may be accessed without charge at the Georgetown University Medical Center Institute for Reproductive Health's website (www.cyclebeads.com). CycleBeads may be purchased for $12.50 on-line and are expected to be available through health-care providers in the near future. If a couple uses the SDM with barrier methods during fertile times, the barrier methods will be an additional cost.

Questions for Conversation

1. What for you is most appealing about the SDM? How does your spouse view this method's advantages?

2. What for you is the SDM's most important drawback? How does your spouse view the disadvantages? Are the disadvantages of the SDM acceptable to you?

3. The SDM prevents pregnancy by requiring abstinence or use of barriers during fertile times. For you, is this an ethically acceptable mechanism of action? Why or why not?

4. The SDM requires daily attention to a woman's cycle. Does this routine suit you?

5. The SDM identifies a fertile time each month. What could you do during the fertile time to express sexual intimacy? Would you use abstinence or barrier methods?

6. The SDM requires cooperation between spouses. How might communication and cooperation work out in your relationship? How might you approach potential difficulties?

7. On a scale of one to ten (one meaning "absolutely not" and ten meaning "this looks really good"), how do you rank this method? How does your spouse rank it?

8. As a couple, do you assess the SDM in a similar way or in different ways? Are any of your disagreements significant enough to warrant consideration of a different method?

7

Withdrawal

Withdrawal (also called coitus interruptus, taking care, or taking precautions) involves removing the penis from the vagina before ejaculation. It prevents pregnancy because sperm are not released into the woman's body.

Mechanism of Action

Withdrawal prevents sperm from entering the woman's body; therefore, the sperm and egg cannot meet. To use withdrawal correctly, a man must know when he is about to ejaculate and be able to remove his penis from the vagina at that point.

Effectiveness

With correct use, about four out of a hundred couples will become pregnant within one year of use. When you add people who sometimes use withdrawal incorrectly, about nineteen out of a hundred couples will become pregnant in a year.[1]

When withdrawal fails, despite correct use, it is because sperm were released into the vagina.[2] An ejaculation occurs at orgasm, and the ejaculatory fluid contains millions of sperm. Men also produce pre-ejaculate, or precum, a small amount of fluid that flows from the tip of the penis during arousal. This is lubricating fluid produced by the Cowper's glands that does not contain sperm. However, sperm still present in the penis or on the skin from previous ejaculations may be in the pre-ejaculate. A man cannot tell when the pre-ejaculate is flowing and cannot control it.

How to Maximize Effectiveness

Use correctly. A man should urinate and wash or wipe off the tip of his penis before intercourse. This will help eliminate sperm that may be present from a previous ejaculation. During intercourse, the man must remove his penis from the vagina before ejaculation. He should ejaculate away from the woman's genitals. Don't underestimate the persistence of sperm—if they are deposited on the woman's vaginal lips or pubic hair, they may travel through the vagina to the egg!

Practice. A couple may practice withdrawal while using another contraceptive method. Some men may learn to do withdrawal correctly, while others are unable to anticipate ejaculation. For both men and women, conscious decision making becomes clouded as orgasm approaches, and many men cannot resist the biological drive to push the penis deeper into the vagina as intercourse progresses.

Do not use withdrawal for repeated acts of intercourse. If a man has more than one orgasm, sperm from the first ejaculation will still be present on and in the penis.

Advantages

Always available. Withdrawal is always available, requires no prescription or doctor's visit, and involves no chemicals or objects that a couple must remember to purchase and have on hand.

Natural. Withdrawal does not affect the body's hormones, uses no chemicals, and has no negative health effects for men. Some myths say withdrawal is psychologically or physically harmful to men, but this is not true.

Involves the male in contraception. Withdrawal allows a man to accept a high degree of responsibility and involvement in contraception.

Chemical free. Couples who cannot or do not wish to use chemicals or other contraceptive technologies may find withdrawal to be appealing.

Reversible. Withdrawal does not affect fertility, so when a couple stops using withdrawal, they may try to become pregnant immediately.

Does not harm the fetus. If a woman becomes pregnant while using withdrawal or after discontinuing use, there is no harm to fetal or infant health.

Disadvantages

Interrupts intercourse. Some couples find withdrawal to be dissatisfying because it requires conscious decision making and moving away from each other just before orgasm, a point at which release of consciousness and moving as close as possible is often desirable. Withdrawal also may decrease sexual pleasure for women and reduce orgasmic intensity for men.[3]

Requires cooperation between partners. Working together to avoid pregnancy may be difficult for some couples.

May not work for all couples. This method may not be possible for men who experience premature or unpredictable ejaculation.

Cost

Withdrawal is free. It does not involve a doctor's visit or any classes.

95

Is Withdrawal a Sin?

Withdrawal is sometimes referred to as onanism or the sin of Onan. Some Christians refer to masturbation or the entire range of sinful sexual behavior as onanism. The story of Onan and his sin is found in Genesis 38, but I'll summarize it here and explain why I do not think the Bible forbids withdrawal.

Onan and Er were sons of Judah and Shuah. Er did something evil, though the Bible doesn't say what, and the Lord killed him. Er's wife, Tamar, was left without a husband or children. A Hebrew woman of that time depended on her husband and sons for her livelihood and stability. For example, in losing her husband, and the possibility of bearing a son, Tamar lost her social standing, financial security, and provisions for the future. In addition, Er's lineage was lost forever. To solve problems like this, the Hebrews practiced levirate marriage. Levirate marriage required a man to marry his brother's widow. The children from this new marriage would belong to the deceased man's lineage. Levirate marriage ensured security for the widow and created a lineage for her deceased husband. The custom was widely practiced in the area and is also mentioned in Ruth 4 and Deuteronomy 25.

When Er died, Onan became the eldest son in his family. As such, he stood to inherit both Er's share of his father's estate and his own share. By providing a son to Tamar, Onan would lose his double inheritance because Er's share, which would have been a substantial amount, would go to Tamar's son.

Judah, Onan's father, told Onan to marry Tamar and produce children, but Onan only pretended to obey. Onan had sex with Tamar numerous times, but the Bible says he "spilled the semen on the ground" (Gen. 38:9). Onan lied and deceived his father, selfishly attempting to get his brother's inheritance. He also abused Tamar, using her sexually and refusing to give her the children she needed. Onan's sins were disobedience, deceit, selfishness, and abuse. The Lord was displeased with Onan and killed him.

Onan practiced withdrawal to retain his double inheritance, but withdrawal itself is not presented as a sin in this story. (Incidentally, Onan may or may not have masturbated to bring himself to orgasm; the text does not make this clear.) In fact, withdrawal was probably widely practiced among the Hebrews and in surrounding cultures, and it is not condemned in Old Testament law nor by Jesus or the early church. Genesis 38 is not about the ethics of any contraceptive method. It is a story about a man who cheated, lied, and deceived his family members to get what he wanted.[4]

Questions for Conversation

1. What for you is most appealing about withdrawal? How does your spouse view this method's advantages?

2. What for you is withdrawal's most important drawback? How does your spouse view the disadvantages? Are the disadvantages of withdrawal acceptable to you?

3. Withdrawal prevents pregnancy by pulling away from each other at a moment of great sexual intimacy. For you, is this an ethically acceptable mechanism of action? Why or why not?

4. Will this method allow you to better express and enjoy sexual intimacy? Why or why not?

5. Withdrawal requires cooperation between spouses. How might communication and cooperation work out in your relationship? How might you approach potential difficulties?

6. On a scale of one to ten (one meaning "absolutely not" and ten meaning "this looks really good"), how do you rank this method? How does your spouse rank it?

7. As a couple, do you assess withdrawal in a similar way or in different ways? Are any of your disagreements significant enough to warrant consideration of a different method?

8

Lactational Amenorrhea
Method

The lactational amenorrhea method (LAM) is a temporary contraceptive method for women who are breast feeding. Breast feeding changes a woman's hormones, making pregnancy unlikely while a baby is given all, or nearly all, nutrition through its mother's milk.

Mechanism of Action

Normal menstrual cycles stop during pregnancy. They resume, on average, forty-five days after birth for a mother who is not breast feeding. Breast feeding, or lactation, extends this period of infertility by changing the brain's hormone production, so the hormone cycles necessary for ovulation do not occur.[1] Infant suckling at the nipple is what triggers these changes.

LAM should only be used by women who are fully, or nearly fully, breast feeding (no bottle feeding and minimal food supplements). LAM reliably prevents pregnancy for six months after birth. Even if a woman menstruates in her first six months of breast feeding, it is very unlikely that the ovulation and endometrial preparation will be sufficient for a pregnancy. Breast pumping does not have the same fertility-inhibiting effect.

Beyond six months, it is more likely that ovulation and menstruation will resume while the woman is breast feeding. The statistics supporting LAM as a reliable contraceptive are based on six months of breast feeding. Women who continue exclusively breast feeding, however, resume ovulation at an average of fourteen and one-half months after delivery.[2] This fact suggests that LAM, when combined with fertility awareness knowledge, may reliably be used beyond six months. A woman must be properly trained in fertility awareness in order to detect the onset of fertility.

Effectiveness

If a woman breast feeds exclusively or with minimal supplemental food and has not experienced a period since the birth of her baby, LAM is 98 percent effective for the first six months following a birth. This means that of one hundred women using LAM correctly for six months postpartum, two will become pregnant.[3]

How to Maximize Effectiveness

Be sure LAM is an appropriate method for you. To use LAM as a temporary contraceptive method, you must be breast feeding around the clock, feeding the baby on demand, avoiding any bottle feeding, and providing minimal supplements by spoon or cup. Use another contraceptive method as soon as food supplements become more than 10 percent of the baby's nutrition (admittedly, this is difficult to measure), when you reduce the frequency or duration of breast feedings, when you resume menstruation, or when the baby is six months old.[4]

Consult a lactation specialist. Hospitals and nonprofit organizations such as La Leche League offer specialized assistance for lactating mothers. A specialist can help you successfully breast feed and can provide advice for your specific situation.

Advantages

Natural. LAM is completely natural and noninvasive. It carries no risk of medical side effects.

Provided by woman's own body. For women who are eligible for this method, LAM is contraception provided by the woman's own body. How convenient! There is nothing to purchase, remember, or monitor.[5]

Reversible. When a woman reduces or stops breast feeding, fertility quickly returns.

Provides other benefits. In addition to enhancing bonding between mother and child, breast feeding benefits infants in many ways. Breast-fed infants are at lower risk for respiratory and gastrointestinal illness, allergies, and sudden infant death syndrome. Their brains, teeth, and immune systems also benefit from breast milk. Breast feeding helps protect women from ovarian, uterine, and breast cancers.[6]

Disadvantages

Learning to breast feed can be difficult for some women. Some women, despite their best efforts, are unable to breast feed. Developing a support network is essential for women who want to use LAM, whether they learn to breast feed or make another choice.

Cost

LAM is free. A woman's body produces milk free of charge, though she should feed her body with healthy foods. Many new mothers find helpful support in books or with lactation consultants, some of whom charge fees.

Questions for Conversation

1. What for you is most appealing about LAM? How does your spouse view this method's advantages?

2. What for you is LAM's most important drawback? How does your spouse view the disadvantages? Are the disadvantages of LAM acceptable to you?

3. Will this method allow you to better express and enjoy sexual intimacy? Might it suppress sexual intimacy? Why?

4. On a scale of one to ten (one meaning "absolutely not" and ten meaning "this looks really good"), how do you rank this method? How does your spouse rank it?

5. As a couple, do you assess LAM in a similar way or in different ways? Are any of your disagreements significant enough to warrant consideration of a different method?

Part 3

Barrier Methods

Condoms

Mechanism of Action

A condom acts as a physical barrier between penis and vagina. Upon ejaculation, the condom retains semen, preventing it from entering the vagina or cervix.

Types of Male Condoms

Consumers have many choices of condoms; over one hundred condoms are on the market in the United States. If particular attributes are important to you, look for them on the condom package before purchase. Following is a discussion of such attributes.

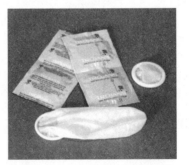

Fig. 9.1. A male condom is an elastic sheath with one closed end; it is placed on the erect penis before intercourse.

Presence or absence of lubrication. Many people desire additional lubrication during intercourse,

105

while others find the smell or taste unpleasant. Lubricants may also be purchased separately and used with condoms.

Spermicidal properties. Experts recommend combining condom use with a spermicide to achieve a higher degree of effectiveness. Most pretreated condoms contain a small amount of nonoxynol-9, a common spermicide. Before purchasing condoms, read the package to see whether or not the condoms inside are pretreated with a spermicide.

Thickness. All modern condoms are very thin, less than .1 mm. They do vary in thickness, however, which may affect physical sensation during intercourse. If either the man or woman experiences loss of sensation during intercourse, purchasing thinner condoms may be an option.

Texture. Condoms are produced with no texture or with texture (ribbed). Some men and women report greater sensation during intercourse with textured condoms, while others report no significant difference.

Color. The basic colors of condoms are transparent, gold, and neutral. Others are brightly colored. The color of a condom does not affect its performance.

Width and length. Condoms vary slightly in their width and length, though they are very elastic and fit most penises. If your penis is particularly large or small, you may ask a medical provider for options. Some condom packages are labeled "large" or "snug" to accommodate various sizes. Some condoms are labeled "baggy," and are worn baggy on the penis. This may increase sensation for some men.

Presence of a reservoir end. A reservoir end is like a nipple at the end of the condom. It covers the tip of the penis and provides ample space for semen upon ejaculation. Nearly all condoms have reservoir ends. If you use a condom without a reservoir end, leave a bit of space at the tip when you put it on.

Novelty condoms. Some condoms are made with novelty colors, materials, attachments, or flavors. Many novelty condoms are not approved for contraceptive use or for protection against sexually transmitted diseases. Read the package or ask a medical provider or pharmacist if you are unsure about the quality

106

of a condom. If a condom is approved for contraceptive use, this will be stated on the package. In general, novelty condoms may be used for intercourse, but they cannot be relied upon for contraception.

Material. Latex condoms are most commonly manufactured in the United States and are sometimes called "rubbers." Latex acts as a barrier for both semen and many sexually transmitted diseases. "Natural skin" condoms (also called "natural membrane" or "skin") are made from the processed tissue from lamb intestines. Natural skin conducts heat better than latex, so these condoms are sometimes considered superior in terms of sensation. Natural skin condoms prevent the transmission of semen but do not protect against numerous sexually transmitted diseases, including hepatitis B virus, herpes simplex virus, and HIV. They are also more expensive than latex condoms. The third type of condom is nonlatex (also called "polyurethane" or "synthetic"). This type is made from various synthetic plastics. These avoid latex allergies, and some have better heat-conducting properties, storage properties, or other traits.[1]

The Female Condom

Only one female condom, named Reality, is currently on the market. It is made of a clear polyurethane plastic, which is nonlatex.[2] Both ends of the condom have a flexible ring that holds the condom in place. The female condom may be used with a spermicide for greater effectiveness.

Effective mness

Condoms can be very effective at preventing pregnancy, but high effectiveness rates depend on proper and consistent use. With correct use of male condoms, about three out of one hundred women will become pregnant in one year of use. When you add people who sometimes use condoms inconsistently or incorrectly ("typical use"), about fourteen out of one hundred women will become pregnant in one year.[3]

107

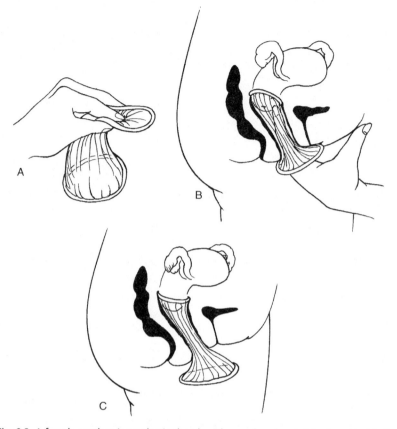

Fig. 9.2. A female condom is an elastic sheath with one closed end; it is placed inside the vagina before intercourse.

With correct use of female condoms, about five out of one hundred women will become pregnant in one year of use. When you add people who sometimes use female condoms inconsistently or incorrectly, about twenty-one out of one hundred will become pregnant.[4]

The significant discrepancy between correct-use rates and typical-use rates exists because effectiveness depends on proper and consistent use. To increase effectiveness, most experts recommend the use of a spermicide with condoms. Except in the case of allergy, spermicides do not increase the already minimal medical risks associated with condoms.[5]

108

How to Maximize Effectiveness

Use condoms every time you have intercourse. One study of teenagers showed a lack of correlation between condom carrying and condom use; teens were carrying condoms but not using them.[6] Purchasing, storing, and carrying condoms are of no use if they are not worn during intercourse!

Wear male condoms correctly. If you have never used a condom before, practice! Prepare to feel silly, and then use a banana, several fingers, or an erect penis to practice condom usage. Unroll the condom a short distance over a finger before placing it on the penis. The rolled rim should always remain on the outside of the condom. Place the condom on the tip of the erect penis like a cap, and roll it down to the base of the penis. Leave one-half inch of space at the tip to collect semen. Add lubrication before intercourse if desired. Withdraw the penis from the vagina soon after ejaculation, while the penis is still hard, holding the rim of the condom against the base of the penis. When the penis is away from the woman's genitals, slowly slide the condom off the penis and discard. When you are first learning to use condoms, keep several nearby during intercourse. If you unroll a condom the wrong way or tear one, do not attempt to fix it or reuse it. Use a new one.

Wear female condoms correctly. To wear a female condom correctly, first squeeze the inner ring (the closed end) to compress the condom. While compressed, insert the condom into the vagina as far as it will go. It can't go too far, and it won't hurt. The condom will stop at the cervix. The outer ring (the open end) should be outside the vagina. Be sure the condom is not twisted inside the vagina. After intercourse, remove the condom before standing up. Twist the open end of the condom closed, and gently pull the condom out of the vagina (see fig. 9.2).

Use only one. Do not use a male condom with a female condom, because neither will work properly. You may use either type of condom with spermicides, other barrier methods, or hormonal methods for greater effectiveness.

Handle condoms carefully. Avoid unrolling, stretching, tugging, or pulling condoms before use. Do not fill a condom with water

109

to test for punctures before use, and do not open the condom package with a sharp object.

Store condoms properly. Condoms are best stored at room temperature in a dry, dark place (a dresser drawer or linen closet is fine). Do not leave condoms in your car; outside in the sunlight; in a humid, wet, or hot room; or near exposure to fluorescent light. Look at the expiration or manufacture date on the package. Do not use a condom that has expired or is five years past its manufacture date.

Never reuse condoms. If a condom has been unrolled the wrong way, do not roll it again and use it. If a condom has been used for intercourse, do not wash it and reuse. Reuse of condoms may spread infection and weakens the condom's strength.

Ensure adequate lubrication. Many couples desire additional lubrication when using condoms. Lubrication problems include using insufficient, excessive, or inappropriate lubricants.[7] The most natural approach to lubrication is to give the woman sufficient time and stimulation to produce her own vaginal lubricants. Additional lubrication may be added according to the directions on the package of lubricant. In general, water-based lubricants are safe for latex condoms, while oil-based lubricants can damage the condom and result in breakage or seepage of semen. Safe lubricants include Aqua-Lube, Astroglide, Condom-Mate, contraceptive foams, creams, and gels, K-Y jelly, and water. Dangerous lubricants include suntan oil, rubbing alcohol, petroleum jelly, butter, margarine, cooking oils, baby oils, and others. Ask a medical provider about other possible lubricants.

Advantages

Readily accessible. Condoms are readily accessible in stores or family planning clinics and do not require medical appointments or follow-up. They are easily purchased, stored, and transported as needed.

Safe. Condoms do not contribute directly to death, infertility, or other serious medical conditions. Their effect on the body is external and temporary, with no lasting effect on the body after use (except in the case of latex allergy).

Provide male, female, or shared responsibility. Unlike other contraceptive methods that rely entirely upon a woman's initiative, the male condom requires male participation. At the very least, a man must agree to wear a condom. A man might also agree to take responsibility for purchasing and remembering to use condoms. If a woman wants control over contraception, the female condom provides this option.

Reversible. Condoms do not affect fertility, and if a couple decides to seek pregnancy, they may do so immediately after stopping condom usage.

Need only be used when required. Condoms may be a good option for infrequent intercourse. They only affect the body during use, unlike hormonal methods that exert systemic effects or self-observation methods that require action daily.

Enhancement of erection. For some men, condoms enhance the strength and duration of an erection. This may be because the condom reduces penile sensation (increasing the time until ejaculation) or because it constricts blood flow at the base of the penis. Condoms do not, however, remedy erectile dysfunction. This condition requires a doctor's care.

STD and HIV protection. Condoms are the best contraceptive option for protection against STDs and HIV. Condoms also protect fertility by guarding against STDs that cause infertility. People who desire such protection sometimes use a condom in addition to another form of birth control.[8]

No harm to the fetus. If a woman becomes pregnant during or after condom use, it will not harm the fetus or infant.

Disadvantages

Female condom is large and cumbersome. The female condom is relatively large, and some people find it visually unappealing or odd. Some women find it difficult or uncomfortable to insert the condom into the vagina. In addition, it can make rustling noises during intercourse.[9]

Sensitivity is reduced during intercourse. Some men and women report reduced sensation during intercourse, while others find

111

condoms do not affect sexual pleasure or sensation. If condoms reduce sensation, try a different texture or brand.

Intercourse is interrupted. Because a condom must be placed on an erect penis, usage usually interrupts foreplay. Some couples are not bothered by this interruption, others make condom usage a creative part of foreplay, and some cannot use condoms because of this interruption. Having condoms close at hand can help minimize the interruption.

Erection may be lost. Some men lose an erection when a condom is placed on the penis. Integrating condom usage into foreplay may help this problem, but some couples are unable to use condoms because of this issue.

Some are allergic to latex. Latex allergies are increasing in frequency, especially among health-care workers who are frequently exposed to it. If you experience burning, itching, pain, cough, rash, hives, chest tightness, shortness of breath, or shock during or after using a latex condom, see a medical professional to be tested for allergies. Latex allergy symptoms may be mild or severe and can be fatal. If you know you have a latex allergy, use non-latex condoms.

Spouses must cooperate with one another. Sometimes people are resistant to condom use due to dislike or misinformation. If condoms are a couple's choice of birth control, they must be used with every act of intercourse to be effective. If either partner is not in agreement, another method will be necessary.

Cost

Male condoms cost from approximately twenty-seven cents to a dollar per condom. If a couple had intercourse two times a week for a year, condoms would cost them between twenty-five and a hundred dollars per year. Female condoms cost approximately three dollars per condom.[10] If a couple had intercourse two times a week for a year, female condoms may cost around three hundred dollars per year. Prices vary by type of condom, quantity in a box, and location. Condoms may be purchased at drug stores, grocery stores, or general stores and do not require a doctor's prescription. They also may be found at family planning clinics for free or at a reduced cost.

Questions for Conversation

1. What for you is most appealing about condoms? How does your spouse view this method's advantages?

2. What for you is the condom's most important drawback? How does your spouse view the disadvantages?

3. Are the disadvantages and medical side effects of condoms acceptable to you?

4. Condoms prevent pregnancy by placing a barrier between sperm and egg. For you, is this an ethically acceptable mechanism of action? Why or why not?

5. Condom use requires ongoing purchase of condoms. Does this suit you?

6. What do you think of placing a physical barrier between you and your spouse during intercourse, prohibiting skin-to-skin contact? Do you think this will impact the physical, emotional, or other intimate aspects of intercourse?

7. How do you each feel about taking responsibility for contraception? Is the man willing to wear a condom? Is the man willing to take other responsibilities (purchasing, remembering to use, etc.)? What responsibilities will the woman take?

8. What if, when using condoms, one person experiences inadequate sexual sensation, function, or pleasure? How will you communicate this?

9. On a scale of one to ten (one meaning "absolutely not" and ten meaning "this looks really good"), how do you rank this method? How does your spouse rank it?

10. As a couple, do you judge the use of condoms similarly or differently? Are any of your disagreements significant enough to warrant consideration of a different method?

10

Spermicides

A spermicide is a chemical that prevents pregnancy by immobilizing or killing sperm so none can reach and fertilize the egg. Spermicide is contained in a gel, foam, or other "carrier" that holds the spermicide within the vagina. Spermicides are often used with a vaginal barrier such as a diaphragm or cervical cap, but they may be used alone.

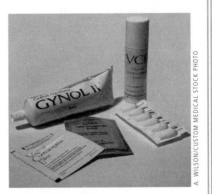

Fig. 10.1. Spermicides come in a jelly, foam, film, cream, or suppository.

Mechanism of Action

Spermicidal products consist of two components: the spermicidal chemical and the substance that holds the chemical, called a "carrier" or "base." Common carriers include gel, foam, cream, film, suppository, tablet, or jelly. In addition to "carrying" the spermicide, some carriers also provide additional lubrication or act as a barrier to sperm in the vagina.

115

The spermicidal chemical is the active agent. When a spermicide comes into contact with sperm, it destroys the cell membrane surrounding the sperm, causing the sperm to die. In the United States, Nonoxynol-9 (N-9) is the most commonly used chemical. Other chemicals are used internationally, and new chemicals are being researched and developed.

Types of Spermicidal Products

Products vary by type of carrier, dose of spermicide, method of application, and length of effectiveness. Products also vary by brand, so it is essential to read the package closely to understand how to use a specific product. Study the following types of spermicidal products to determine which will best suit your needs.

Suppositories. A suppository is a tablet or other solid object that is inserted high into the vagina, touching the cervix. It dissolves, releasing the spermicide into the vagina. It becomes effective about fifteen minutes after it is inserted and effectiveness lasts for approximately one hour. A suppository may be used alone or with a condom.

Gel, Cream, Jelly, or Foam. Gel, creams, jellies, and foam are inserted into the vagina with a plunging device shaped like a tampon applicator. The applicator must be pushed far into the vagina so the spermicide covers the cervix. They become effective immediately, and their contraceptive effect lasts for approximately one hour. Gel, creams, and jellies are usually marketed for use with a diaphragm, cervical cap, or condom, but they may be used alone.

Film. Vaginal contraceptive film is a two-inch paper-thin square that is inserted into the vagina, covering the cervix. It melts, releasing spermicide into the vagina. It becomes effective approximately ten to fifteen minutes after insertion and lasts for approximately one hour. Vaginal contraceptive film may be used with a diaphragm, cervical cap, condom, or by itself. Placing film on the end of the penis before intercourse is not recommended because it may not reach the cervix or cover it sufficiently, and because the film is not immediately effective.

116

Effectiveness

Effectiveness research on spermicides is not as conclusive as research on other methods. There is greater variation in reported effectiveness rates for spermicides than for any other method. Information on the package of a specific product may be helpful in deciding whether an effectiveness rate is sufficient for your needs.

With correct use, about six out of one hundred women will become pregnant in one year of use. With typical use, about twenty-six will become pregnant in one year.[1]

Medical professionals advise using spermicides with another method such as a condom, cervical cap, or diaphragm. Using a physical barrier and a spermicide increases effectiveness.

How to Maximize Effectiveness

Use consistently. To achieve maximum effectiveness rates, spermicides must be used every act of intercourse.

Use according to directions. After purchasing a spermicidal product, carefully read the package instructions. If you have questions, consult a medical professional. Spermicidal products differ in the way they are used, when they become effective, and how long their effectiveness lasts. Be sure that you understand when and how it should be placed in the vagina, how long to wait before intercourse, and when its effectiveness decreases. Most spermicides should remain in place (with a diaphragm or cap) for at least six hours after intercourse. Be sure to use enough spermicide. If more than one hour has passed between insertion and intercourse, use another application.

Do not make your own spermicide. Websites or friends may recommend homemade spermicides involving fruit jellies, hair gels, lemon, acidic foods, or cosmetic chemicals. Even if a chemical or food seems similar to a spermicidal product, do not use it. Homemade spermicides are not as effective as medical spermicides, and they may cause serious physical harm.

117

Do not douche after sex. Douching with water, or even with a spermicide, may wash sperm toward the uterus and fallopian tubes.

Keep supplies on hand. Be sure to have spermicidal products available for any ejaculation that takes place in or near the woman's vagina. Running out of supplies is a frequent reason couples fail to use spermicides.

Take care of supplies. Keep spermicidal products in a clean, cool, dark place. Wash reusable applicators with soap and warm water. Again, follow package instructions. If an applicator is disposable, do not use it more than once. If a product has exceeded its expiration date, do not use it.

Advantages

Medical side effects are minimal. No long-term or serious medical side effects are associated with the use of spermicides. Researchers continue to explore possible long-term systemic effects, which at this point seem to be minimal.[2]

Responsibility for use may be shared. If a woman wants full responsibility over contraception, she may purchase and use spermicides by herself. If a couple wants to share responsibility, the man may take responsibility for purchasing spermicides while the woman takes responsibility for using them.

Effects are not permanent. Fertility returns immediately after the spermicidal effect wears off.

Fetus is unharmed. If a woman becomes pregnant while using spermicides or after discontinuing use, there is no harm to fetal or infant health.

Need only be used when required. Spermicides may be a good option for infrequent intercourse. They affect the body only when used for intercourse.

Some protection against sexually transmitted diseases is offered. This benefit is strongest when spermicides are used with condoms. Spermicides alone are an insufficient protection against STDs.

118

They are a good backup. If you are concerned about your regular method (forgot to take a pill, worried about slippage of IUD, etc.), spermicides may provide a good backup.

They provide some lubrication. A noncontraceptive benefit of spermicides is that they provide additional sexual lubrication.

Disadvantages

Some people are allergic or sensitive. This is the most common problem associated with spermicides. If you experience pain, itching, or discomfort after using a spermicide, see a medical professional. Sometimes a couple may use a different type of spermicide or carrier; sometimes they have no choice but to use a different method.

Infections. Spermicides are associated with a risk of vaginal and urinary tract infections. See a doctor if you experience pain, burning, itching, or discomfort.

Correct technique may be difficult to learn. Some users may find it difficult or embarrassing to insert spermicides. These difficulties may be resolved through practice or by consulting a medical professional.

Some dislike them in general. Some users find the taste and smell of spermicides to be unpleasant. During intercourse, some users may feel a gritty sensation if the spermicide is not fully melted or dissolved. Other users perceive spermicidal use to be messy and inconvenient.

Vaginal anatomy must be normal. Abnormal vaginal anatomy may interfere with placement or retention of spermicide. If a woman has abnormal anatomy, she should consult a medical professional before using spermicides.

Sexual intimacy may be interrupted. Vaginal spermicides must be inserted shortly before intercourse, which may interfere with sexual spontaneity.

May not prevent STDs. Researchers once believed that spermicides helped prevent several STDs, but newer research suggests that it does not protect against chlamydia, gonorrhea, or

119

HIV.[3] Research on spermicides and STDs is ongoing and not yet conclusive.

Cost

Prices for spermicides vary greatly by type, brand, and location of store. Prices per use may vary from thirty cents to a dollar. If a couple has intercourse twice a week for a year (104 times in a year), spermicides may cost between thirty and a hundred dollars. Most spermicides are sold at a drug store or general store, so you can easily make cost comparisons for your area.[4]

Questions for Conversation

1. What for you is most appealing about spermicides? How does your spouse view this method's advantages?
2. What for you is spermicides' most important drawback? How does your spouse view the disadvantages?
3. Are the disadvantages and medical side effects of spermicides acceptable to you?
4. Spermicides prevent pregnancy by immobilizing or killing sperm. For you, is this an ethically acceptable mechanism of action? Why or why not?
5. Spermicides require ongoing purchase of supplies. They also require touching the woman's genitals and using an applicator or finger to insert the spermicide. Is this a routine that suits you?
6. Will this method allow you to better express and enjoy sexual intimacy? Will it suppress sexual intimacy? Why?
7. On a scale of one to ten (one meaning "absolutely not" and ten meaning "this looks really good"), how do you rank this method? How does your spouse rank it?
8. As a couple, do you assess spermicides in a similar way or in different ways? Are any of your disagreements significant enough to warrant consideration of a different method?

11

Vaginal Barriers

Diaphragm, Sponge, and Cervical Cap

Vaginal barriers are contraceptive devices inserted into the vagina. They prevent pregnancy by stopping the sperm from entering the cervix. Vaginal barriers include the diaphragm, cervical cap, sponge, and female condom. (For information about the female condom, see chapter 9.)

Mechanism of Action

Diaphragms, caps, and sponges work in two ways: they provide a physical barrier that prevents sperm from entering the cervix, and they hold a spermicide that kills sperm. The female condom covers the entire vagina and cervix, and may be used with or without a spermicide. For greatest effectiveness, vaginal barriers may be used with spermicides.

Types of Vaginal Barriers

Diaphragm

The diaphragm is a shallow rubber cup with a flexible rim. A woman places spermicide inside the diaphragm and inserts it high into the vagina. It covers the cervix, and the pubic bone structure holds the diaphragm in place. Once inserted, the diaphragm is effective for six hours. If more than six hours pass before intercourse takes place, a new application of a spermicide is needed, though the diaphragm need not be removed. The initial application of a spermicide is put inside the diaphragm, and subsequent applications are put into the vagina, covering the outside of the diaphragm. After intercourse the diaphragm should be left in place for approximately six hours but not more than twenty-four hours. There is a risk of toxic shock syndrome if it is left in place for too long. After removal, the diaphragm is washed and stored for reuse.

Diaphragm purchase requires a medical visit and fitting. A medical professional can help determine the best type of diaphragm and fit your body with the correct size.

The Lea Contraceptive is a new diaphragm-like device that covers the cervix. It is a one-size-fits-all silicone barrier that does not require a doctor's visit for use. It is available from the manufacturer and may be purchased on-line or over the counter in Germany. In the United States it has not been approved by the FDA.[1]

Cervical Cap

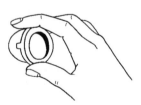

The cervical cap is a deep rubber cup with a firm, round rim. A woman places a spermicide inside the cap and inserts it high into the vagina. The cap seals around the base of the cervix. It provides effective contraception for forty-eight hours after insertion, regardless of how many times intercourse occurs. No additional spermicide is necessary. Like the diaphragm, the cervical cap should not be worn longer than its recommended time. After removal, the cap is washed and stored for reuse.

One cervical cap is currently available in the United States, though more options are available in other countries. The Prentif Cavity-Rim Cervical Cap (also called Prentif) is made of latex rubber and is available in four sizes. A doctor fits a woman for the proper size.

Oves is a new type of contraceptive cap. It has not been approved by the FDA in the United States, but it is available online and over the counter in France. It is a disposable silicone cap that may be worn for three days. It comes in three sizes, and a woman may purchase several caps and take them to a health-care provider for proper fitting.[2]

FemCap is a second new type of contraceptive cap, also made of silicone. It is designed for easier insertion and removal and has an attached strap to facilitate removal. FemCap is still being researched and may be available soon.[3]

Sponge

The contraceptive sponge is a small sponge containing spermicide. One side of the sponge has a dimple that rests against the cervix. The other side has a loop that allows for easy removal. A woman moistens the sponge with tap water and inserts it high into the vagina.

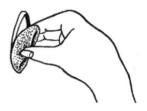

It provides effective contraception for up to twenty-four hours regardless of how many times intercourse occurs. After intercourse, the sponge must be left in place for at least six hours but not more than twenty-four hours.

Contraceptive sponges may be purchased over the counter and do not require a doctor's visit. In the United States the Today Sponge was a popular method until the mid-1990s when, for financial reasons, the manufacturer ceased production. Production of the Today Sponge in the United States resumed in 2002.

They soon will be released in Canada and later in the United States. The Protectaid sponge and the Pharmatex sponge are available in Canada and Europe. Sponges are not available over the counter in the United States, but they may be purchased on-line.[4]

Effectiveness

Measuring the effectiveness of vaginal barriers is complex because effectiveness varies for different women. Important factors include a woman's fertility, the frequency of intercourse, and whether or not the woman has had a baby. For a woman who has had a baby, the sponge and cap are less effective than the diaphragm. For a woman who has not had a baby, the three barriers are equally effective. Women who have not had a baby, are over thirty, and do not have intercourse frequently are most likely to avoid accidental pregnancy with a vaginal barrier. Younger women who have intercourse frequently are more likely to become pregnant, as are women who have had a baby.[5]

Diaphragm. With correct diaphragm use, about six in one hundred women will become pregnant in one year of use. When you add women who sometimes use the diaphragm incorrectly, about twenty will become pregnant in one year. These rates are the same regardless of whether or not a woman has ever had a baby.

Cervical cap. Among users of the cervical cap who have not had a baby and use the cap correctly, about nine will become pregnant in one year of use. When you add women who sometimes use the cap incorrectly, about twenty will become pregnant. Among users of the cervical cap who have had a baby and use the cap correctly, about twenty-six will become pregnant in one year of use. When you add women who sometimes use the cap incorrectly, about forty will become pregnant.

Sponge. Among users of the sponge who have not had a baby and use the sponge correctly, about nine will become pregnant with perfect use. When you add women who sometimes use the sponge incorrectly, about twenty will become pregnant. Among users of the sponge who have had a baby and use the sponge correctly, about twenty will become pregnant in one year of use.

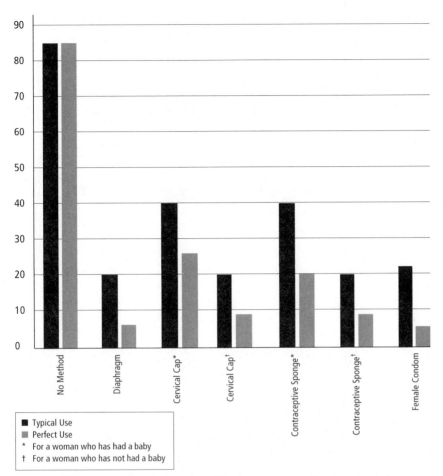

Fig. 11.1. Effectiveness of Vaginal Barriers. This chart represents the percentage of women experiencing an unintended pregnancy in the first year of continuous typical or perfect use.

When you add women who sometimes use the sponge incorrectly, about forty will become pregnant.

How to Maximize Effectiveness

Use consistently. Vaginal barriers must be used with every act of intercourse to achieve the highest effectiveness rates possible. One common reason for method failure is inconsistent use.

Use correctly. Common problems include not applying additional spermicide with additional acts of intercourse, removing the barrier too soon after intercourse, or not using spermicide with the barrier. Talk with your medical provider about the correct use of a diaphragm or cap, and read the label instructions on spermicidal foam or jelly.

Keep supplies on hand. Sometimes a couple occasionally fails to use a barrier because they do not have supplies on hand.

Take care of supplies. Store your contraceptive supplies in a dark, cool place. Clean them according to labeling or doctor's instructions. Never put oil-based lubricants (mineral oil, baby oil, suntan oil, vegetable oil, or butter) on a latex product. They may harm the effectiveness of a condom, diaphragm, or cap. Each time you use a diaphragm or cap, inspect it visually for cracks, holes, or tears.

Advantages

Convenient. Diaphragms must be fitted, and inserting vaginal barriers requires some learning. After these preliminaries are taken care of, however, vaginal barriers become a quick and easy contraceptive method.[6]

Minimal side effects. Vaginal barriers are noninvasive and do not alter a woman's hormonal patterns.

Couples may share responsibility for contraception. If a woman wants or needs to be in control of contraception in her sexual relationship, vaginal barriers allow this. If a couple wants to share responsibility, the man may purchase spermicide or check the barrier for cracks, holes, or tears.

Reversible. Fertility is unaffected by vaginal barriers and returns immediately upon removal of devices.

Need only be used when required. Vaginal barriers can be a good option for people who have intercourse infrequently.

Can be inserted before time of intercourse. For a couple that wants a barrier method but is dissatisfied with the presence or interruption of a condom during intercourse, diaphragms, caps, or sponges may provide a good option.

126

Some STD protection. When used with spermicides, risks from some sexually transmitted diseases may be reduced. Vaginal barriers cannot, however, be relied upon as sure protection against STDs or HIV. In a test tube, spermicides kill many organisms that cause STDs. In the human body, however, these lab results have not been consistently replicated.

Fetus is not harmed. If a woman becomes pregnant while using a barrier method, or after discontinuing use, no harm to fetal or infant health will result.

Disadvantages

Some people experience unpleasant side effects. The most common problem reported by vaginal barrier users is skin irritation, and other problems include spermicide allergies, cramps, bladder pain, or rectal pain. Some rare cases of vaginal abrasion or laceration have been reported. Some men have reported penis pain during intercourse from pushing against the diaphragm or cap. Refitting the device may resolve some of these problems. In addition, foul odor and vaginal discharge are likely to occur when a vaginal barrier is left in place beyond its recommended time. Symptoms cease when the device is removed. Some sponge users report vaginal dryness or difficulty in removing it.

Can interrupt sexual intimacy. Because vaginal barriers must be inserted before sexual intercourse, they may hinder sexual spontaneity.

Some people are allergic to latex. Latex allergies usually cause painful reactions in the vagina or on the penis, and in some serious cases latex allergy can cause death. If a person knows that he or she has a latex allergy, he or she should consult with a doctor. A doctor can offer plastic alternatives to some latex contraceptives.

Barrier methods are associated with vaginal and urinary tract infections. Spermicides, when used alone, with male condoms, or with vaginal barriers, are associated with a higher risk of vaginal and urinary tract infections. Pressure of the diaphragm or cap against the cervix may also be a contributing factor. See a doctor if you

127

experience infections (pain, burning, itching, discomfort), and if symptoms occur with frequency, you may need to use a different spermicide or a different contraceptive.

Toxic Shock Syndrome (TSS) is a rare side effect. TSS is a rare but serious disorder usually associated with tampon use, but it may also be caused by vaginal barrier use. The risks are low: approximately two to three cases of TSS per year are reported per one hundred thousand vaginal barrier users in the United States. These cases result in less than one death per one hundred thousand users annually. If you use a vaginal barrier, you should familiarize yourself with TSS and its symptoms. See a doctor if you experience high fever, vomiting, diarrhea, dizziness, weakness, rash, sore throat, or aching muscles.[7]

Cost

The cost of a doctor's visit and fitting for a diaphragm or cap ranges from $50 to $150, depending on your location and insurance. Purchase of the diaphragm or cap itself is around $40. Replacement is recommended every two years for a diaphragm and every year for a cap. Purchasing spermicidal foam or jelly is an ongoing cost for vaginal barriers, and this cost depends on frequency of intercourse. Spermicides generally cost around $.25 per application, though they are sold in tubes or cans containing many applications.

When purchased on-line, the Protectaid sponge costs about $3.50 per sponge. The Lea Barrier is $58 (reusable), and the Oves cap is about $6 (wear one for three days and then dispose).[8]

Questions for Conversation

1. What for you is most appealing about vaginal barriers? How does your spouse view this method's advantages?

2. What for you is vaginal barriers' most important drawback? How does your spouse view the disadvantages?

3. Are the disadvantages and medical side effects of vaginal barriers acceptable to you?

4. Vaginal barriers place a physical barrier between sperm and egg. The spermicides used with barriers kill sperm. For you, is this an ethically acceptable mechanism of action? Why or why not?

5. Use of vaginal barriers requires purchase of devices and spermicide, a doctor's visit (some do not require this), and attention to proper use. They also involve touching the woman's genitals to insert the barrier. Is this a routine that suits you?

6. Who will take responsibility for purchasing and caring for contraceptive supplies? Might you be able to share responsibilities? How?

7. For your relationship, what might it mean to place a barrier between you during sex? Might the barrier diminish intimacy? Might the reassurance against unexpected pregnancy enhance intimacy? How else might a barrier impact your relationship?

8. On a scale of one to ten (one meaning "absolutely not" and ten meaning "this looks really good"), how do you rank this method? How does your spouse rank it?

9. As a couple, do you assess barrier methods in a similar way or in different ways? Are any of your disagreements significant enough to warrant consideration of a different method?

Part 4

Hormonal Methods

12

Combined Hormonal Contraceptives

The Pill, Injections, Patch, and Vaginal Ring

Combined hormonal contraceptives are called "combined" because they prevent pregnancy by delivering a combination of estrogen and progestin to a woman's body. The pill, or birth control pill, is the most commonly used combined hormonal contraceptive. New methods using the same hormones include monthly injections, the contraceptive patch, and the vaginal ring.

Mechanism of Action

Combined hormonal contraceptives deliver synthetic hormones to a woman's body that affect the body in many ways, some unrelated to pregnancy prevention.[1] The hormones prevent pregnancy in three ways.[2] First, they prevent ovulation.

133

Most of the time no egg is matured and released, so pregnancy is not possible. Second, the hormones thicken cervical fluid, immobilizing sperm. Sperm are unable to complete their travel to the fallopian tubes, making fertilization impossible. Third, they alter the development of the endometrium, making it thinner and less tacky. This may prevent a fertilized egg from implanting in the uterus.[3]

The various types of combined hormonal contraceptives (pill, injection, patch, vaginal ring) work the same way. They prevent ovulation most of the time. Changes in the cervical fluid and endometrium are "back-up" contraceptive mechanisms that function on the rare occasion that the woman ovulates.[4]

Types of Combined Hormonal Contraceptives

Birth Control Pill

Many brands of birth control pills are available. They vary in the quantity of hormones they contain, though all birth control pills currently on the market have hormone dosages much lower than in the past. They also vary in that some maintain a steady 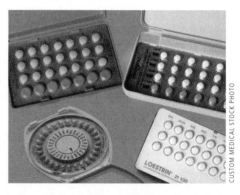 dose of hormones ("monophasic"), while others deliver doses to the body in two ("biphasic") or three ("triphasic") phases throughout a monthly cycle. Most pill users take one pill every day. For three weeks, the pills carry hormones, and for one week the pills are placebos (sugar pills). Most women menstruate during the hormone-free week. Many women try more than one brand of pill before finding one that is suitable. A doctor will help determine which type of pill is best, given a woman's medical history, current health condition, and experience of side effects.

Commonly prescribed combined oral contraceptives include Alesse, Loestrin, Estrostep, Ortho Tri-Cyclen, Triphasil, and

Nordette. Relatively new combined oral contraceptives include Yasmin and Cyclessa. A new pill called Seasonale could be on the market in the United States in 2003. This pill allows a woman to bleed just three to four times a year rather than monthly.[5]

Injections

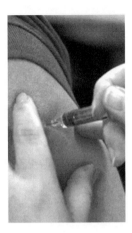

Combined hormonal injections deliver hormones to the body through a shot given in the arm, thigh, or buttock. Injections must be updated monthly with the time between injections not exceeding thirty-three days.

A monthly injection called Lunelle was the first combined hormonal injection available in the United States.[6] Combined hormonal injections have been available in other countries for many years under names including Cyclofem and Cyclo-Provera. Injections commonly used in the United States, such as Depo-Provera, contain only progestin and are not combined hormonal methods (Depo-Provera is covered in the next chapter).

Contraceptive Patch

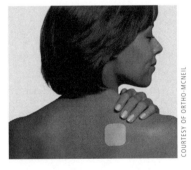

The contraceptive patch is a small square adhesive patch. It is placed on the lower abdomen, buttocks, or upper body (but not on the breasts or on any broken or irritated skin). The patch has three layers that carry contraceptive hormones which are slowly released into the bloodstream through the skin. The patch is worn for one week and then replaced with a new patch. The woman does this for three weeks and then does not wear a patch the fourth week. This induces bleeding. The woman's hormonal changes and her withdrawal bleeding are the same as if she were taking a birth control pill.[7] The patch became available to U.S. consumers in 2002.[8]

135

Vaginal Ring

The vaginal ring is a flexible, soft ring approximately two inches across and one-eighth of an inch thick. A woman places it around her cervix, high in the vagina. It is easy to insert and does not have to be placed in a precise part of the vagina. It stays in place comfortably and does not cause pain during intercourse.[9]

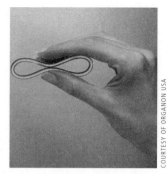

COURTESY OF ORGANON USA

The ring releases hormones that prevent pregnancy. It is worn for three weeks and removed for one week of withdrawal bleeding. This schedule of three hormone weeks and one hormone-free week is the same as most contraceptive pills. The vaginal ring, brand name NuvaRing, became available to U.S. consumers in 2002.[10]

Effectiveness

All combined hormonal methods are highly effective. Rates differ slightly for the various delivery systems, but all are around 99 percent effective when used correctly.

Pill. With correct use (i.e., for those who miss no pills and follow instructions perfectly), less than one in one hundred women will become pregnant in one year of use. When you add people who sometimes use the pill incorrectly, about five in one hundred women will become pregnant in one year.[11]

Injection. With correct use (i.e., for those who update their injections at the proper time), less than one in one hundred will become pregnant in one year of use.[12] Typical-use rates are not yet available because injections are new.

Patch. With correct use (i.e., for those who wear and replace the patch correctly), less than one in one hundred will become pregnant in one year of use.[13] Typical-use rates are not yet available because the contraceptive patch is new.

Vaginal ring. With correct use, about one or two in one hundred women will become pregnant in one year of use.[14] Typical-use rates are not yet available because the ring is new.

136

How to Maximize Effectiveness

Give an accurate medical history to your health-care provider. Combined hormonal contraceptives are not a wise choice for every woman, and a doctor can help determine whether or not combined hormones are a good option for you. Conditions such as obesity, smoking, and age are important factors, and in addition some medications reduce the effectiveness of combined hormonal contraceptives.[15]

Use consistently and correctly. Each type of combined hormonal contraceptive has a routine that must be followed to be effective. The pill must be taken at the same time every day, the patch and ring must be worn for three weeks and removed for one week, and injections must be updated monthly. If you forget to take a pill, wear a ring or patch, or update a shot, you should use a condom or another barrier method. Each method has procedures for resuming correct use if the user fails to follow the schedule. Save brochures and package inserts about your method for referral. One study showed that only 12 percent of those who used the pill could correctly explain how to take it and what to do if they forgot to take it.[16] This information is important when you miss a day, as most women occasionally do.

Have a back-up plan. Many unexpected pregnancies occur when a woman decides to discontinue a method and does not have another contraceptive plan. Nearly 50 percent of women using combined hormonal contraceptives switch methods within the first year, so if you experience negative side effects or are planning to discontinue combined hormonal contraceptives, be sure to have another plan that you will use immediately.

Advantages

Most research has been done on the birth control pill because it has been on the market longer than the patch, injections, or vaginal ring. However, all of these hormonal contraceptives deliver the same hormones to the body, so most advantages are the same for all methods.[17]

137

Convenient. Many women appreciate the convenience of daily or long-lasting contraception.

Women can control or share responsibility for contraception. For women who want or need control of contraception, combined hormonal contraception provides this advantage. For couples who want to share responsibility, a man and woman may divide the responsibilities of purchasing, remembering, and using the method.

Reversible. Combined hormonal contraception is a reversible form of birth control, with no lasting effects on fertility or on a fetus. When use is stopped, most women will menstruate again and be able to have a healthy baby. Because women's bodies readjust to natural hormones at different rates, it may take a woman additional months to become pregnant after coming off the pill. In a study of seventy combined hormonal injection users who discontinued use to get pregnant, 50 percent of the women were pregnant within six months, and 82.9 percent were pregnant within twelve months.[18] These pregnancy rates are similar for women who did not use hormonal contraceptives. Other studies have shown combined hormone users to conceive slightly later than nonusers.

Don't interrupt intercourse. Many couples appreciate methods that do not interfere with foreplay or intercourse.

Monthly menstruation. Women who take combined hormonal contraceptives menstruate (also called "withdrawal bleeding") when hormones are withdrawn from the body during the pill-free or placebo week.[19] Because the levels of hormones in these contraceptives are so low, they can result in several benefits for women, such as diminishing cramps and pain, decreasing the length and intensity of bleeding, and decreasing the risk of anemia. Some women experience diminished premenstrual symptoms, but in rare cases the symptoms intensify. Women may also have some control over when menstruation begins by taking hormone pills for additional days.[20] Consult with a doctor before regulating the time of menstruation, because the process is different for various brands and types of contraceptives.

Other noncontraceptive health benefits. Pill users experience reduced risks for ovarian cancer—up to an 80 percent reduced risk for women who use the pill for twelve or more years.[21] For women with a family history of ovarian cancer, pill use may significantly reduce the risk of contracting the disease.[22] Combined hormonal contraceptives also reduce a woman's risk for endometrial cancer, ectopic pregnancy, functional ovarian cysts, benign breast disease, and acute pelvic inflammatory infection. They are also used as treatment for several medical conditions, including acne, painful menstruation, hirsutism (excess body hair), and dysfunctional uterine bleeding.[23]

Disadvantages

In addition to preventing pregnancy, synthetic hormones exert systemic effects on the body. Women consider some of these changes desirable, such as reduction of acne and less pain during menstruation, while other changes are irritating, unpleasant, or dangerous. It is important that a woman or couple learn about potential harms associated with any birth control method. Even when the risks are slight, they are risks.[24]

As with the advantages of this method, most research related to medical side effects has been done on the birth control pill. Harms related to hormone use are likely similar for injections, patch, and vaginal ring because they deliver similar hormones. Some disadvantages, however, are specific to a method's delivery system.

Require regular attention. Combined hormonal methods require attention on a daily, weekly, or monthly basis.

Unpleasant side effects. Relatively common side effects include breast enlargement and overall bloating due to water retention, depression, diminished sex drive, gingivitis, hair loss, hair gain, headaches, nausea, menstrual disruption (scanty bleeding, missed periods, breakthrough bleeding), vaginal discharge, and cervical changes.[25] Sometimes these side effects last for a few cycles and then disappear, while others persist. Some women gain weight while using combined hormonal contraceptives; others lose weight.[26] Less common but potentially serious side effects include vomiting, cramps and pains in legs, and urinary infections.

Fifty percent of first-time pill users discontinue use within the first year, and over 30 percent switch types or brands within the first year.[27] The most common reason for discontinuation of the pill and other combined hormonal methods is unpleasant side effects. A woman is even more likely to stop using a method if she experiences more than one side effect. For many women, their sense of sexuality and self-image are strongly affected by their weight and mood, which is why these unpleasant side effects can become unbearable.[28] Fear of side effects is another reason for discontinuation.[29]

May delay return of fertility. Combined hormonal contraception is a reversible form of birth control, but fertility's return may be delayed for some users. One large study showed that 90 percent of previously fertile women conceived within thirty months after coming off the pill, conceiving two to three months later than their counterparts who did not use the pill. For women of ages thirty to thirty-five, the delay is longer, though six years after discontinuation, fertility rates were the same for women in this age group who had used the pill and women who had not.[30]

May affect the cardiovascular system. The most serious complications associated with pill use are stroke, blood clots, and heart attack.[31] The risk of cardiovascular complications is heightened for women who have other risk factors for heart problems: sedentary lifestyle, overweight, over thirty-five years of age, diabetic, high blood pressure, smoker, high cholesterol, or history of heart disease.

Strokes are extremely rare among women of childbearing age, occurring in approximately eleven of one hundred thousand women per year. Women who smoke or have a history of hypertension are at higher risk for strokes. The research on combined hormonal contraceptives and strokes is difficult to interpret because much of it was conducted before lower doses of hormones were available in birth control pills. Pills currently available, all of which contain relatively low doses of hormones, minimize the increased risk of stroke. For these reasons, combined hormonal contraception is considered safe for women who do not otherwise have risk factors for a stroke.[32]

Heart attacks are also rare among women of childbearing age. The risk of heart attack for combined hormonal contraception users seems to be highest for women who smoke or who are over age thirty-five and smoke or who have other risk factors for heart attacks. The estimated risk of heart attack associated with combined hormonal contraception use among nonsmokers is three per one million women each year.

The risk of blood clotting in veins (also called venous thromboembolism or VTE) associated with pill use is fewer than three per ten thousand women per year (the rate is one per ten thousand in nonpill users). The pill causes a small but significant risk of VTE.[33]

The pill is also correlated with an increased risk of high blood pressure, which predisposes a person to other heart and circulatory diseases.[34] Blood pressure often returns to normal when hormone use ceases.[35]

May increase risk of breast cancer. Some studies have concluded that risk of breast cancer may increase for women who are younger than thirty-five when they use combined hormones and for women who use them for many years. The risk increases 24 percent while women are using the hormones, and the risk gradually decreases to zero ten years after use is discontinued. The prevalence of breast cancer in women under age thirty-five is small, however, with or without hormonal contraception.[36]

May increase risk of liver disease. Combined hormonal contraceptives are associated with liver tumor, jaundice, and gallstones. These risks are low; the risk of a liver tumor, for example, is one in one hundred thousand users per year.

Possible problems with injections. Irregular bleeding may occur during the first three months of use. Severe allergic reactions are also possible.[37]

Possible problems with the contraceptive patch. In one study, 5 percent of women had a patch that did not stay attached to the skin, and 2 percent withdrew from the study due to skin irritation from the patch.[38] In clinical trials for FDA approval, other side effects experienced by women included breast symptoms, headache, nausea, menstrual cramps, and abdominal pain.[39]

Possible problems with vaginal ring. The vaginal ring carries a small risk of vaginal infection, irritation, and discharge.

If you experience any of the symptoms below (ACHES), see a medical professional immediately.[40]

A — abdominal pain
C — chest pain
H — headache, dizziness, weakness, numbness
E — eye problems (vision loss or blurring)
S — severe leg pain in calf or thigh

Cost

The cost of birth control pills varies with geography and insurance. Without insurance, on an annual basis generic pills cost approximately $100 to $130, and nongeneric pills cost approximately $200 to $300. Public clinics may be able to offer pills at a reduced cost or free.[41] The birth control patch, injection, and vaginal ring are comparable in price.

Do Hormonal Methods Cause Abortion?

People who oppose hormonal methods argue that they are wrong for several reasons. First, they say the side effects and medical risks of hormonal contraception are too great. Women may experience unpleasant side effects, serious medical harm, or even death. Some Christians interpret this risk as poor stewardship of the body and choose methods with lesser risks. Second, some people oppose hormonal methods because they damage marriages. These Christians say that hormonal methods allow a couple to trust technology more than they trust God in their sexual relationship. In addition, when sex is always available (i.e., when there is never a need for abstinence), the virtues of self-control and attentiveness to a woman's cycle are lost.

A third argument, one that is most persuasive to Christians who are otherwise inclined to use hormonal methods, is that these methods may cause abortion. Natural family planning authors John and Sheila Kippley claim that nearly two million conceived human lives are aborted each year by the pill. Medical doctor Chris Kahlenborn testified to the FDA that "a woman who takes the oral contraceptive pill will have at least one abortion for every year that she is on it."[42] The same argument is made about Norplant, Depo-Provera, and other brands of hormonal contraceptives. Millions of pro-life Christians use the pill, however, and most doctors tell patients that hormonal methods are a safe, effective birth control option.

How can a Christian understand this controversy and develop a personal stance? Christians on either side of the issue often insist that their moral position is clear and well evidenced. Unfortunately, it really is a murky issue with conflicting and incomplete information.

I want to show you both sides of the issue—why some Christians say hormonal methods are abortive, and why others say they are not. I wish I could conclude this chapter with a crystal-clear answer to the question, Do hormonal methods cause abortion? Unfortunately, I can't offer such an answer, but perhaps I can provide you with a better understanding of the details of this dilemma.

Because the heart of the issue is about the termination of life, it might seem that understanding the way hormonal contraceptives work would answer our question. No such luck! Even this is complicated. Hormonal methods prevent pregnancy by over-riding the body's natural hormones with synthetic hormones that affect the body in many ways, three of which are contraceptive. First, hormonal contraceptives prevent ovulation, preventing an egg from reaching maturity. Second, they change the cervical fluid—a substance produced by the cervix that nourishes and provides transport to sperm. Third, they weaken the uterine lin-

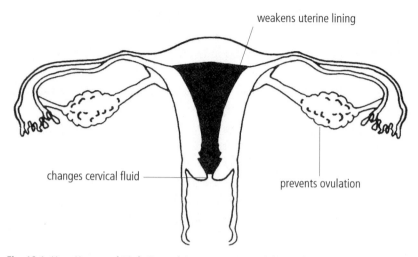

weakens uterine lining

changes cervical fluid

prevents ovulation

Fig. 12.1. How Hormonal Birth Control Acts on a Woman's Reproductive System. Hormonal methods affect the reproductive system in three ways: preventing ovulation, changing the cervical fluid, and changing the endometrium.

ing, which may make the uterus inhospitable to a fertilized egg, preventing implantation.

The abortion question focuses on the weakening of the uterine lining; does this prevent a fertilized egg from implanting in the uterus? In a woman who is not taking hormonal contraception, the endometrium builds up each month, becoming thick, tacky, and filled with blood and nutrients necessary for a fetus's nourishment. If a woman becomes pregnant, it is because an egg was fertilized in the fallopian tubes, moved through the tubes to the uterus, "stuck" to the tacky uterine lining, and began to grow. Synthetic estrogens and progestins change the uterine lining, making it thinner and relatively slippery. If a woman who is taking hormonal contraceptives ovulates (a rare occurrence) and if the egg is fertilized (even more rare), it may be unable to implant in this weak, underdeveloped endometrium.

For Christians who believe that life begins at conception, any method that prevents pregnancy after conception is ethically problematic. The antiabortion American Life League argues, "The chemicals [in the pill] can prevent a human embryo from implanting in the mother's uterine lining. 'That's abortion,' said

[Judie] Brown [president of the American Life League]. 'It kills a living human being in his earliest stages of development.'"[43]

Other Christians disagree with these conclusions and say the pill has not been proven conclusively to be an abortifacient (an abortion-causing agent). Four Christian doctors wrote the following: "The abortifacient theory [about the pill] is not a fact. It fails to account for the essential information about ovulation and its effect on the uterine lining." The weakened uterine lining has been observed in pill-taking women who did *not* ovulate. It's possible that if a pill-taking woman does ovulate, ovulation itself will stimulate other hormones to prepare the endometrium quickly for implantation. About seven days pass between ovulation and implantation, which may give the endometrium time to "catch up," making a successful pregnancy possible. Indeed, some women do become pregnant while using hormonal methods, and they carry and deliver healthy babies. These doctors conclude that while a theoretical risk of abortion exists with hormonal methods, it is not a known risk and so does not carry the ethical weight of a known risk. They confidently counsel Christian patients to use hormonal contraception without fear of abortion.[44]

It's confusing when experts reach opposing conclusions that are based on the same medical research. Unfortunately, the abortifacient issue is not a high priority for research funders, so gathering data about these internal, microscopic biological processes is difficult. Christians on both sides agree that it is ethically wrong to end a life after it has begun. Both sides are also confident in their assessment of hormonal methods as either abortifacient or not.

If this issue is important to you and you are considering hormonal contraception, look closely at your method of choice and at your own routine. For example, if a woman uses combined hormonal pills with perfect regularity, there is a very small chance that she will ovulate. Therefore, the abortifacient properties of the pill are not likely to come into play. Most women, however, miss a few pills per month. If the missed pills are during the middle of her cycle, a woman may ovulate. In this case, the weakened uterine lining may play an abortifacient role if the egg is fertilized. A woman may resolve this issue by trying to take the pill without fail. Should she miss a pill or two, she can use another form of contraception or abstain for several days.

For the most part, the ethical issues surrounding combined hormonal contraceptives and progestin-only contraceptives are the same. It is important to realize, however, that about 50 percent of women who take the minipill (progestin-only pill) continue to ovulate regularly. With this method, pregnancy is avoided primarily by thickened cervical fluid that blocks sperm movement. If, however, an especially persistent sperm survives and fertilizes the egg, the uterine lining may prevent the pregnancy from continuing. Implants (Norplant and others) and injections (Depo-Provera and others) prevent ovulation nearly always, so the abortifacient issue is not as strong for these methods.

Perhaps an accurate though dissatisfying conclusion is that it is possible that hormonal methods prevent a fertilized egg from continuing its development on the rare occasion when a woman using a hormonal method ovulates and her egg is fertilized. Some women and couples may find that this risk warrants use of other contraceptive methods, while others may comfortably use hormonal methods until more conclusive evidence emerges.

Questions for Conversation

1. What for you is most appealing about combined hormonal contraception? How does your spouse view this method's advantages?

2. What for you is combined hormonal contraception's most important drawback? How does your spouse view the disadvantages?

3. Are the disadvantages and medical side effects of combined hormonal contraception acceptable to you?

4. Combined hormonal contraception prevents pregnancy by altering a woman's hormonal patterns. In addition, it may prevent a fertilized egg from implanting in the uterus. For

you, is this an ethically acceptable mechanism of action? Why or why not?

5. The pill requires consistent use, taking the pill at the same time each day. Could you follow this routine? How will you and your spouse work together to ensure correct and consistent use?

6. Will this method allow you to better express and enjoy sexual intimacy? Might it suppress sexual intimacy? Why?

7. On a scale of one to ten (one meaning "absolutely not" and ten meaning "this looks really good"), how do you rank this method? How does your spouse rank it?

8. As a couple, do you assess combined hormonal contraception in a similar way or in different ways? Are any of your disagreements significant enough to warrant consideration of a different method?

13

Progestin-Only
Contraceptives

Minipill, Injections, and Implants

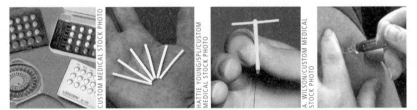

Fig. 13.1. Progestin-only contraceptives may be delivered to the body in a pill, implant, hormonal IUD, or injection.

Progestin-only contraceptives deliver hormones to the body in a pill, implant under the skin, intrauterine system (IUS), injection, or possibly in the future a vaginal ring.[1] Progestin-only contraceptives prevent pregnancy by delivering progestin, a synthetic progesterone, to a woman's body.

Mechanism of Action

Progestins exert numerous effects on the body, several of which are related to prevention of pregnancy. Progestins often suppress ovulation, though not as consistently as combined hormones. Progestins also thicken cervical fluid, preventing sperm from reaching the fallopian tubes. Lastly, they may prevent implantation of a fertilized egg by slowing the movement of a fertilized egg through the fallopian tubes and by weakening the uterine lining.

Injections. Injections prevent pregnancy primarily by suppressing ovulation. They also thicken cervical fluid and weaken the uterine lining.[2]

Implants. Implants suppress ovulation in at least half of a woman's cycles. When a woman ovulates, other hormonal changes most likely prevent fertilization.

Minipills. Minipills contain a very low dose of hormones, and they act in women's bodies in different ways. Most of the time the minipill works by thickening the cervical fluid to hamper sperm movement. It may also weaken the endometrium to prevent implantation. The minipill stops ovulation in around 50 percent of the women who use it.[3]

IUS. The IUS (also called the hormone-releasing IUD) prevents pregnancy in multiple ways. It thickens cervical fluid, weakens the endometrium, slows the movement of a fertilized egg through the fallopian tubes, and prevents ovulation. The IUS is covered in more detail in chapter 15.

Types of Progestin-Only Contraceptives

Injection. A medical professional gives a woman a shot of progestin in her buttock or upper arm, and she returns for a new shot every three months. Depo-Provera is the most commonly used injection in the United States, though others are available.[4]

Implants. A doctor implants a number of soft match-sized rods underneath the skin of a woman's inner arm. These rods release small quantities of progestin into the bloodstream. They are effective for a particular amount of time and must be removed and reinserted by a medical professional.[5] Norplant implants are most widely used in the United States. This system consists of six rods, effective for five years. New, innovative implants that are or may soon be available include Norplant II/Jadelle (two implants, three to five years of use), Implanon (effective for one to three years), Capranor (effective for two years), Uniplant (one implant), and Elcometrine (effective for six months).[6]

Minipill. Minipills are similar to other birth control pills, but they are called minipills because they contain smaller hormonal doses. Each progestin-only pill contains the same hormone, and there are no pill-free days for a woman who is using the minipill. Brand names of minipills include Microlut, Micronor, and Ovrette.

Effectiveness

Injections. With correct use (i.e., the doctor correctly administers injections and the woman updates them on time), less than one in one hundred women will become pregnant in one year of use. Because the effectiveness of injections lasts for several months, effectiveness rates for correct use and typical use are the same.

Implants. With correct use (i.e., the doctor correctly administers the implants and the woman updates them on time), less than one in one hundred women will become pregnant in one year of use. Because the effectiveness of implants lasts for a year or more, effectiveness rates for correct use and typical use are the same.

Minipills. With correct use (i.e., for those who take the pill at exactly the same time every day), less than one in one hundred women will become pregnant in one year of use. When you add women who sometimes use the method incorrectly, approximately five in one hundred will become pregnant.[7]

How to Maximize Effectiveness

Give an accurate medical history to your health-care provider. Progestin-only contraceptives are often good choices for breastfeeding women, older women, young women, and women who cannot take estrogen. For women with certain conditions including diabetes, heart problems, breast cancer, and other health problems, they may be an unwise choice. In addition, some medications reduce the effectiveness of these contraceptives. Even if you take an antibiotic or other medication for a brief period of time, inform your health-care provider or pharmacist.

Use consistently and correctly. Read the package insert or product brochure and talk with your medical provider about using the method correctly. Minipills must be taken with nearly perfect regularity because they contain low doses of hormones that do not last long. Implants must be removed and replaced, and injections require regular updates. A woman or couple must develop a routine that will remind them of these schedules. Some product websites offer e-mail reminders.

Have a back-up plan. Many unexpected pregnancies happen when a woman goes off a hormonal contraception and does not have another plan in place. If you experience negative side effects or choose to stop using a progestin-only contraceptive for another reason, it is helpful to have a back-up plan in place.

Advantages

Convenient. Many women consider daily or long-lasting contraception to be convenient.

Offer no estrogenic side effects. Women who cannot be exposed to estrogen or have experienced estrogen-related side effects may use progestin-only contraceptives. The heart-related complications associated with estrogen are not associated with progestins.[8]

Woman can control or share responsibility for contraception. If a woman wants or needs control of contraception, progestin-only methods provide this advantage. If a couple wants to share responsibility, a man can remind the woman to take her pill or remind the woman of implant or injection updates.

Reversible. Fertility returns after use of progestin-only contraception is discontinued. After stopping use of implants, women become pregnant at rates equal to nonimplant users, and no negative effects on fetal, infant, or maternal health result.[9] Injections are reversible after the effects of the last shot wear off, though ovulation may not return until nine to ten months after the last shot. Progestin-only contraceptives do not harm a fetus or infant.

Do not interrupt intercourse. Progestin-only methods do not interfere with foreplay or intercourse.

May stop menstruation and menstruation-related problems. Progestin-only contraceptives make women bleed much less or stop menstruating entirely. This often decreases cramps and anemia. Injections are likely to eliminate bleeding, especially as a woman uses them for multiple years, though injections often cause significantly heavier bleeding for the first several months. Implants often eliminate menstruation within six months. This side effect is least likely for the minipill because many users continue to ovulate. Some women consider menstrual changes to be an advantage, while others consider them a disadvantage.[10]

Noncontraceptive benefits. Progestin-only contraceptives may protect against endometrial cancer, decrease benign breast disease, and reduce the risk of ectopic pregnancy. Injections may also reduce sickle crises in women with sickle cell anemia.[11]

May be used during breast feeding. Progestin-only contraceptives may be used safely during breast feeding. Some doctors recommend waiting until a baby is six months old, while others prescribe progestin-only contraceptives sooner.

Disadvantages

Disadvantages of All Progestin-Only Methods

Require regular attention. Progestin-only contraceptives require attention on a daily, weekly, or monthly basis.

Menstrual cycle may be disturbed. Many women experience more days of spotting or light bleeding or cease menstruation altogether. This is a common reason for discontinuing use of this method.

Side effects are unpleasant. Many women experience unwanted side effects that result in discontinuation of the method. These side effects vary for each progestin-only method.

Disadvantages of Injections

Unpleasant side effects. Women may experience heavy menstruation in the first months of use, insomnia, acne, headache, bloating, swelling of hands or feet, backache, leg cramps, nausea, vaginal discharge or irritation, breast swelling and tenderness, excessive hair loss, lack of hair growth, rash, hot flashes, joint pain, yellowing of the skin, headache, nervousness, abdominal pain, dizziness, increased or decreased sex drive, depression, stomach pain or cramps, fatigue, weakness, or development of dark spots on the skin.[12] Weight gain is another unwanted side effect (a woman using Depo-Provera may gain five pounds in the first year, eight pounds after two years, and twelve pounds after four years of use).[13]

Rare side effects. In rare cases injection users may experience convulsions, jaundice, urinary tract infections, allergic reactions, fainting, paralysis, osteoporosis, infertility, deep vein thrombosis, pulmonary embolus, breast cancer, or cervical cancer.[14]

Upon discontinuation, fertility does not return immediately. If a woman experiences negative side effects, she must wait until the injection clears her system. Fertility does not return immediately upon discontinuation and may take six to twelve months to return to normal. One study showed that among women who stopped using Depo-Provera in order to get pregnant, 50 percent became pregnant within ten months, and 93 percent were pregnant within eighteen months.[15]

"Bad" cholesterol levels may increase. Some studies show levels of HDL cholesterol ("good" cholesterol) fall, and levels of LDL cholesterol ("bad" cholesterol) increase significantly in women using injections.

Bone density may decrease. Long-term injection users may develop decreased bone density. Like all other women, injection users are encouraged to be mindful of their calcium intake and exercise.[16]

Risk of breast cancer may increase. Some studies have shown that injections may accelerate the development of breast cancer, while other studies have shown no association between injections and breast cancer.

Some women experience allergic reactions. A few women are allergic to injections. The effects of the injection cannot be immediately reversed, so these women may take antiallergy medication until the injection wears off.

See a doctor immediately if you experience repeated, painful headaches; heavy bleeding; coughing up blood; frequent urination; depression; severe abdominal pain; or pus, pain, or bleeding at the injection site.[17]

Disadvantages of Implants

Unpleasant side effects. Unpleasant side effects may include headaches, enlargement of ovaries, dizziness, breast tenderness, nervousness, nausea, acne, dermatitis, breast discharge, change in appetite, weight gain, and hair growth or loss.[18]

Weight gain. Over five years, the weight gain among implant users averages around five pounds, which is fairly normal for women in their reproductive years.

Removal may be difficult. Insertion and removal require a minor surgical procedure that sometimes causes discomfort or pain. Be sure that your medical provider is experienced in implant removal. In the early 1990s, problems related to difficult removals resulted in a decline in Norplant use in the United States. Since that time, new implant technologies and greater medical experience with insertion and removal have reduced this problem.[19]

Implant site may become infected or inflamed. One study showed that about 5 percent of users had skin irritation at the implantation site, and less than 1 percent experienced infection or expulsion of an implant.[20] Sometimes the skin over the implant darkens.[21]

See a doctor immediately if you experience severe abdominal pain, heavy vaginal bleeding, arm pain, pus or bleeding at the insertion site, expulsion of an implant, migraine headaches, painful headaches, or blurred vision.[22]

155

Disadvantages of Minipills

Requires daily attention. A woman must remember to take the pill each day.

Hard to find. It can be difficult to find a pharmacy or clinic that prescribes and stocks minipills.

Disrupt menstruation. Minipills often cause extended spotting, light bleeding, or unpredictable bleeding. Some women who take the minipill may need to wear light pads every day.

See a doctor immediately if you experience abdominal pain, repeated and severe headaches, or if you took the pill too late (even three hours late).

Cost

Injections. Annual costs for Depo-Provera are approximately $140. Costs include four injections during the year and office visits.

Implants. A woman pays $500 to $700 for a set of Norplant implants. While this initial cost is high, no additional contraceptive costs are necessary for five years. Additional costs apply for removal of implants.

Minipills. Minipills cost anywhere from $100 to $300 per year, depending on whether they are generic or brand name. Public clinics may offer lower fees.[23]

Questions for Conversation

1. What for you is most appealing about progestin-only contraceptives? How does your spouse view this method's advantages?

2. What for you is progestin-only contraceptives' most important drawback? How does your spouse view the disadvantages?

3. Are the disadvantages and medical side effects of progestin-only contraceptives acceptable to you?

4. Progestin-only contraceptives prevent pregnancy by altering a woman's hormonal patterns. They may also prevent a fertilized egg from implanting in the uterine lining. For you, is this an ethically acceptable mechanism of action? Why or why not?

5. Progestin-only contraceptives require daily or periodic attention, including taking a pill or seeing a doctor for implants or injections. Does this routine suit you?

6. Will this method allow you to better express and enjoy sexual intimacy? Might it suppress sexual intimacy? Why?

7. On a scale of one to ten (one meaning "absolutely not" and ten meaning "this looks really good"), how do you rank this method? How does your spouse rank it?

8. As a couple, do you assess progestin-only contraceptives in a similar way or in different ways? Are any of your disagreements significant enough to warrant consideration of a different method?

Emergency Contraception

An emergency contraceptive is a device or drug that prevents pregnancy after intercourse. Emergency contraception does not terminate an established pregnancy, though it may prevent a fertilized egg from implanting in the uterus. Options include special doses of birth control pills or insertion of an IUD.

Types of Product and Mechanism of Action

Emergency contraceptives are often offered to women who have been raped as well as women who experience a condom break, some other contraceptive failure, or unprotected intercourse for any reason. If you see a doctor for advice after having unprotected intercourse, he or she may suggest emergency contraception as an option.

Emergency contraception is controversial for Christians in large part because it is often called the "morning-after pill,"

159

and it is confused with RU-486, a drug used for early-term abortions. In medical terms, a pregnancy begins when a fertilized egg implants itself on the uterine wall. When a woman uses pills or surgery to end a pregnancy after this point, it is an abortion. Emergency contraception intervenes in the reproductive process before this point and, depending on when it is taken, prevents pregnancy in various ways. While medical professionals define the beginning of pregnancy at successful implantation, Christians often define the beginning of *life* at an earlier point. See the heading "Do Hormonal Methods Cause Abortion?" in chapter 12 for more reflection on this issue.

Emergency Contraception Pills (ECPs)

ECPs are often referred to as the "morning-after pill," which is a misleading nickname because they may be taken up to seventy-two hours after intercourse for maximum effectiveness. They are also misunderstood as "abortion pills." ECPs are not abortion pills; they are totally ineffective after a pregnancy has been established (i.e., when a fertilized egg has implanted in the uterus).[1]

ECPs are usually taken as two doses of birth control pills (either combined hormones or progestin-only) within seventy-two hours of unprotected intercourse. A doctor must prescribe the quantity of pills because dosage varies widely across the various brands of birth control pills. If taken before ovulation, the pills interrupt the development of the maturing egg, preventing or delaying ovulation. This is the best understood effect of ECPs and is believed to be the primary way that ECPs work.[2] They continue to be effective when taken after ovulation, though researchers do not understand this with precision. They may immobilize sperm in thickened cervical fluid, slow the movement of the egg through the fallopian tubes, or prevent a fertilized egg from implanting in the uterus.[3]

Currently, Plan B (progestin-only) and Preven (combined hormones) are the two ECP kits sold specifically for emergency contraception in the United States. Doctors also prescribe special doses of regular birth control pills.[4]

160

RU-486 (Mifepristone)

RU-486 is a different drug than ECPS. RU-486 contains a hormone that acts against progesterone, stopping ovulation and slowing the growth of the uterine lining.[5] If it is taken before ovulation, it prevents ovulation. If taken after ovulation, it prevents a fertilized egg from implanting in the uterus. If taken after a fertilized egg has implanted in the uterus, it terminates a pregnancy. The FDA-approved use of RU-486 is to terminate a pregnancy, but doctors sometimes prescribe it as emergency contraception to be used in a nonabortive way. It is a complex drug that may or may not be abortive, depending on when after intercourse it is taken.

Copper-Releasing IUDs

Inserting a copper-releasing IUD shortly after unprotected intercourse changes the uterine lining or makes fertilization less likely. When used as emergency contraception, the IUD prevents pregnancy by immobilizing sperm and preventing the implantation of a fertilized egg.

Effectiveness

Emergency contraceptives are highly effective but not as effective as consistent use of a regular contraceptive. A couple should not rely on emergency contraception for regular use and should begin using another method immediately after emergency contraception use. The effectiveness of ECPs is highest when used within seventy-two hours of intercourse.[6]

Progestin-only pills. Use of progestin-only pills reduces the risk of pregnancy by almost 90 percent. If one hundred women had unprotected intercourse while in the middle of their cycle, about eight would become pregnant. If they all used progestin-only ECPs, only one would become pregnant — a 90 percent reduction in pregnancy risk.[7]

161

Combined oral contraceptives. Use of combined ECPs reduces the risk of pregnancy by 75 percent. If one hundred women had unprotected intercourse while in the middle of their cycle, about eight would become pregnant. If they all used combined ECPs, only two would become pregnant—a 75 percent reduction in pregnancy risk.[8]

Copper IUD. Use of the copper IUD reduces the risk of pregnancy by over 99 percent. If one hundred women had unprotected intercourse while in the middle of their cycle, about eight would become pregnant. If they all used copper IUDs, less than one would become pregnant—a better than 99 percent reduction in pregnancy risk.[9]

How to Maximize Effectiveness

Plan ahead. If you think you may ever use emergency contraception, talk with a doctor before an emergency arises. Currently, ECPs require a prescription, and you may fill the prescription ahead of time and have ECPs on hand. The American Medical Association supports an initiative to seek FDA approval for over-the-counter use of ECPs, which may come into use in the future. An IUD must be inserted by a medical professional, but you may educate yourself about IUDs in advance.

Use correctly. ECPs come with very specific instructions in the package, or you may receive a doctor's instruction verbally. Follow the instructions; taking extra pills will not increase the method's effectiveness. ECPs are most effective within seventy-two hours of intercourse, so act quickly after intercourse to use them. Copper IUDs may be inserted up to five days after intercourse.

Do not have unprotected intercourse in the days and weeks following use. Continue using a regular birth control method for each act of intercourse.

Use another method consistently. Emergency contraception is effective, but the best way to avoid pregnancy consistently is to use a nonemergency birth control method.

162

Advantages

ECPs

Provide options in an emergency. If for any reason intercourse occurred without contraception or a contraceptive method failed, emergency contraception provides an option for pregnancy avoidance.[10]

No serious medical side effects. Some women who should not use hormonal contraception on a regular basis may use emergency contraception. Exposure to hormones is minimal and the hormones do not exert long-term effects on the body. Women who should not use combined hormones due to heart complication risks may consider progestin-only ECPs.

Reversible. Use of ECPs does not affect future fertility. If a woman takes ECPs and becomes pregnant, the pills will not harm the fetus or the woman.

Copper IUDs

No additional risks beyond regular IUD use. Use of an IUD carries some risks, but using it as an emergency contraceptive does not contribute additional risk.

Reversible. Fertility returns upon removal of the IUD, and its use will not harm a fetus.

Can become a long-term contraceptive. After insertion for emergency contraceptive purposes, the IUD is usually used as a long-term contraceptive.

Disadvantages

ECPs

Interruption of menstrual cycle. A woman's next menstruation may be early, on time, or late. Bleeding may be heavier or lighter than usual.

Unpleasant side effects. The most commonly reported side effects are nausea (50 percent of women studied) and vomiting (5 to 25 percent of women studied). Other side effects include breast tenderness, fatigue, headache, abdominal pain, and dizziness.[11] These side effects subside within a day or two after the pills are taken.[12]

May cause blood clots in legs. The most serious side effect of using combined hormonal pills as emergency contraception is blood clots in the legs, which may be mild or severe. This side effect has not been reported with use of progestin-only pills. Women who have risk factors for heart disease are more likely to experience blood clots than women without risk factors.

See a doctor immediately if you experience chest pain, coughing up blood, severe pain in the calf, sudden severe headache, weakness, numbness, faintness, sudden difficulty in seeing or speaking, severe stomach pain, or jaundice.

Copper IUDs

May be inserted incorrectly. When inserted incorrectly, the IUD may be painful and may perforate the uterus.

Unpleasant side effects. IUD insertion sometimes results in abdominal discomfort and vaginal bleeding or spotting.

Cost

Emergency contraception pills (Plan B and Preven) cost approximately twenty to twenty-five dollars at pharmacies. They may be available at public clinics for free or reduced cost. Other brands of birth control pills prescribed for emergency use may cost up to fifty dollars.[13]

Questions for Conversation

1. What will you do if for any reason you are at risk for an unintended pregnancy?

164

2. What for you is most appealing about emergency contraception? How does your spouse view this method's advantages?

3. What for you are emergency contraception's most important drawbacks? How does your spouse view these disadvantages?

4. Are the disadvantages and medical side effects of emergency contraception acceptable to you?

5. Emergency contraception may prevent a fertilized egg from implanting in the uterus. For you, is this an ethically acceptable mechanism of action? Why or why not?

6. If you plan ever to use emergency contraception, does your doctor prescribe it? Identify a contact clinic and phone number ahead of time.

7. On a scale of one to ten (one meaning "absolutely not" and ten meaning "this looks really good"), how do you rank this method? How does your spouse rank it?

8. As a couple, do you assess emergency contraception in a similar way or in different ways? Are any of your disagreements significant enough to warrant consideration of a different method?

Part 5

IUDs

Intrauterine Devices

Nonhormonal and Hormonal

The intrauterine device (IUD) is a medical object placed in the uterus with marker strings that extend down into the vagina. It prevents pregnancy by interfering with sperm viability and transport, fertilization, and implantation.

The intrauterine system (IUS) is an IUD that includes a slow-release hormone system. It releases low doses of a synthetic progesterone directly into the uterus on a daily basis. It prevents pregnancy in the same ways as an IUD and also by the effects of progesterone.

Fig. 15.1. The IUD is shaped like the letter "T" and is placed inside the uterus. IUDs have been made in many shapes over the years, but IUDs currently in use look like this.

Mechanism of Action

The IUD works primarily by preventing fertilization. First, the IUD immobilizes sperm, interfering with their movement toward the egg. Second, it speeds the movement of the egg through the fallopian tubes, shortening the time that the egg is available for fertilization. IUDs also may change the uterine lining, preventing a fertilized egg from implanting. This second feature of IUDs is an important issue for many Christians, but unfortunately the scientific evidence does not allow a firm conclusion as to whether or not the IUD is an abortifacient.[1]

Some nonhormonal IUDs contain copper. Scientists do not understand the exact way that copper acts as a contraceptive, but it seems to interfere with sperm viability and transport, the fertilization process, and implantation.[2]

The IUS works in the same way as the nonhormonal IUD, and in addition it releases progesterone. The contraceptive effects of progesterone are not perfectly understood, but it seems to incapacitate or kill sperm and alter the uterine lining to prevent implantation. A woman using an IUS will continue to ovulate, but she will likely stop menstruating due to the lack of endometrium build-up.[3]

Types of IUDs and IUSs

Many types of IUDs are available internationally. One IUD and two IUSs are currently available in the United States. Your medical provider can help determine which one is best for you.

Copper IUD (brand name Paragard T 380A, also called "Copper T"). The Copper IUD is a small T-shaped device placed inside the uterus. The vertical part of the T is wrapped with copper wire, and the horizontal arms have copper bands that release small quantities of copper ions over time. The Copper IUD is the most frequently used IUD in the United States. It may be left in place for up to twelve years.

Intrauterine systems. Like an IUD, the IUS is a small T-shaped device placed inside the uterus. It does not contain copper. Rather, a type of progesterone is released from its vertical arm. Two brand names are the Progestasert IUD (effective for one year) and Mirena (effective for five years).

Effectiveness

All IUDs are highly effective in preventing pregnancy. When used correctly (i.e., when a doctor correctly inserts the IUD and a woman checks it regularly), less than one out of one hundred will become pregnant in one year of use. When you add women who use the method incorrectly, pregnancy rates are slightly higher, but still less than one out of one hundred will become pregnant in one year.[4]

How to Maximize Effectiveness

Before Insertion

Seek an experienced doctor. Be sure your medical provider has inserted IUDs frequently in recent months or request a referral to a clinic where IUDs are inserted frequently.

Accurately describe your health history to a medical provider. Your provider may suggest another method depending on your pregnancy status, date of last childbirth, sexually transmitted diseases, menstrual history, general medical history, and number of sexual partners. IUDs are best for women who have had at least one child, are in a mutually monogamous relationship, and have no history of pelvic inflammatory disease.

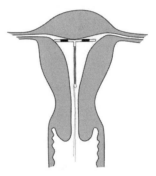

Fig. 15.2. IUD Placement. A doctor inserts the IUD into the uterus. It rests at the top of the uterus, and the marker strings hang down into the vagina.

After Insertion

Check the strings. Your medical provider will teach you how to check the IUD marker strings that extend into the vagina. Be sure you feel comfortable doing this and that you know how often to do it.

171

Treat infections promptly. If you experience pain, fever, severe cramping, or unusual vaginal bleeding, see a doctor immediately. Infections from IUDs may be serious and life threatening if left untreated.

Keep information about your IUD in a reliable place. Remember the dates of follow-up clinic visits and the date for removal of the IUD.

Advantages

Convenient. The IUD's contraceptive effect is long lasting and does not require day-to-day attention.

Allows female control. If a woman wants or needs control over contraception, the IUD provides this advantage.

Reversible. The IUD is nearly always reversible. If a woman has pelvic inflammatory disease (PID) at the time of insertion, the IUD can carry an infection into the uterus and cause infertility. The IUD itself, however, does not cause PID or infertility.

May improve menstruation. The progesterone-releasing IUS often decreases menstrual blood loss and the intensity of painful menstruation. Some types of IUSs can eliminate menstruation completely, which may be perceived as either an advantage or disadvantage.[5]

Noncontraceptive health benefits. The IUS may be used by post-menopausal women on estrogen therapy to protect against endometrial cancer. It also may successfully treat excessively heavy menstruation.[6]

Disadvantages

May cause vaginal irritation. The IUD strings that hang into the vagina may be irritating to women and their sexual partners. This can usually be remedied by asking a doctor to trim the strings.

Increased risk of pelvic inflammatory disease. IUDs may increase the risk of pelvic infection by allowing bacteria to move from the vagina into the uterus during insertion. The IUD does not cause PID; rather, its strings may provide a conduit for infections already present in the body. Cases of PID that develop more than four months after insertion are likely due to intercourse with an infected partner, not from the IUD.[7] PID can result in infertility, hysterectomy, or in rare cases death.

May be expelled. An IUD may spontaneously expel itself from the uterus.[8] This may be painful, but often it happens without the woman noticing it. Checking the IUD strings regularly is the best way to avoid this disadvantage. Women who are young, have an abnormal amount of menstrual flow, or painful periods before IUD use are most likely to experience expulsion.[9]

May be embedded. An IUD may embed itself into the endometrium and require surgical removal.

May cause menstrual disturbance. Ten to fifteen percent of IUD users have their IUDs removed because of menstrual problems. Problems include midcycle spotting or bleeding, increased menstrual flow, or elimination of menstruation.[10] Most women who request IUD removal due to menstrual problems had similar problems before they used an IUD.[11]

May complicate pregnancy. Half of pregnancies occurring with the IUD in place end in miscarriage. If the IUD is removed early in pregnancy, the miscarriage rate is approximately 25 percent. Approximately 5 percent of women pregnant with an IUD in place will have an ectopic (tubal) pregnancy.[12] If a woman continues a pregnancy with the IUD in place, she is at higher risk for premature labor, miscarriage, and fetal damage. If the IUD is removed, there is an increased chance of miscarriage during the procedure, but after that point there are no lasting effects on the fetus.

May perforate the uterus or cervix. Approximately one in one thousand women experience perforation, a condition in which the IUD punctures the uterus or cervix.[13]

IUS may cause other problems. The IUS may cause hormonal side effects including depression, acne, headache, and breast tenderness.[14]

Many of these problems have early warning signs that can be detected. If you experience any of these symptoms listed below (PAINS), see a doctor.[15]

173

P — Period late, abnormal spotting or bleeding
A — Abdominal pain or pain with intercourse
I — Infection, abnormal vaginal discharge
N — Not feeling well, fever, chills
S — String missing, shorter, or longer

Cost

The cost of an IUD or IUS involves a clinic visit, the device itself, the insertion process, and a lab fee. The cost could be $150 to $400, depending on type of clinic and geographic location.[16]

Do IUDs Cause Abortion?

Many Christians avoid IUDs because they believe or suspect they cause abortions. The ways intrauterine devices affect the body are complex and somewhat mysterious, which makes a definitive statement about the IUD's abortive effects difficult. The hormone-releasing IUS works like both an IUD and a hormonal contraceptive, so the ethical issues related to the IUS are doubly complex.

The IUD works primarily by preventing fertilization, like other contraceptive methods. Most of the time pregnancy is avoided because the IUD kills or immobilizes sperm, thus preventing them from reaching the egg. The IUD also prompts a foreign-body response within the uterus, apparently making the uterine lining more slippery and less conducive to implantation. If an egg is fertilized with an IUD in place, the IUD may prevent it from implanting once it reaches the uterus. Prevention of implantation is believed to be a back-up or secondary mechanism of action. Some researchers believe prevention of implantation never happens, while others think it is a possibility.

Research has shown IUDs cause changes in the endometrium, but scientists have not actually observed a fertilized egg being expelled from the uterus. Some scientists believe that if an egg is fertilized while using an IUD, the body's hormonal response will prepare the uterine lining to be favorable to implantation. Indeed, women who use IUDs do sometimes become pregnant and successfully bear children.

Unfortunately, this issue is not of high priority to those who fund research, so firm conclusions about this secondary mechanism of the IUD do not exist. The answer to the question, Do IUDs cause abortion? is a dissatisfying maybe. Some Christians may feel comfortable using this technology until more conclusive evidence emerges, while others may want to avoid even the possibility of disturbing life after conception.

Questions for Conversation

1. What for you is most appealing about the IUD? How does your spouse view this method's advantages?

2. What for you is the IUD's most important drawback? How does your spouse view the disadvantages?

3. Are the disadvantages and medical side effects of the IUD acceptable to you?

4. IUDs prevent pregnancy by immobilizing sperm and possibly by preventing a fertilized egg from implanting in the uterus. For you, is this an ethically acceptable mechanism of action? Why or why not?

5. The IUD requires a doctor's fitting and regular string checks (i.e., touching the marker strings with a finger). Does this routine suit you?

6. Will this method allow you to better express and enjoy sexual intimacy? Might it suppress sexual intimacy? Why?

7. On a scale of one to ten (one meaning "absolutely not" and ten meaning "this looks really good"), how do you rank this method? How does your spouse rank it?

8. As a couple, do you assess the IUD in a similar way or in different ways? Are any of your disagreements significant enough to warrant consideration of a different method?

175

Part 6

Permanent
Methods

16

Male and Female
Sterilization

Sterilization is permanent birth control and is available for both men and women. Vasectomy, the sterilization option for men, involves an operation in which a doctor closes the vas deferens, the tubes that carry sperm from the testes to the penis. Within a short time after a vasectomy, sperm are no longer present in ejaculatory fluid, so a couple cannot become pregnant. Tubal ligation, the sterilization option for women, involves a procedure that blocks the fallopian tubes. This prevents an egg from traveling through the tubes to meet sperm.

Male Sterilization

Mechanism of Action

A vasectomy prevents pregnancy by blocking sperm from traveling their usual route from the testicles into ejaculatory fluid (also called semen). Sperm normally travel through two tubes called the vas deferens, mixing with other seminal fluids to form semen. A vasectomy blocks the vas deferens, which means that after a vasectomy, the testes will continue to produce sperm, but they will simply be reabsorbed by the body rather than traveling out of the body in ejaculate.

A vasectomy does not disrupt a man's hormonal system or his sexual performance. A man's erections, muscle quality, voice, facial hair, and libido (sex drive) will be the same after a vasectomy, as will the appearance of his penis and scrotum. Sperm make up a very small part of ejaculate, so a man's ejaculations will not be noticeably different.

Types of Male Sterilization

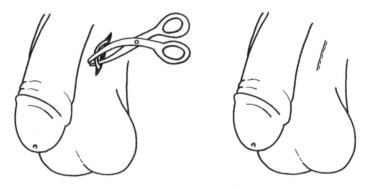

Fig. 16.1. A vasectomy involves severing the vas deferens through a small incision. After surgery, a small scar is left behind.

From a surgical point of view, a vasectomy is a fairly simple procedure that carries low risks. Vasectomy does not require a hospital stay, though a man will need to rest and care for the surgical site afterward.

The two most common types of vasectomies are surgical and "no-scalpel."[1] In a surgical vasectomy, a medical practitioner, often a urologist, applies local anesthetic and makes one or two incisions (about one to two centimeters long) in the scrotum. Inside the scrotum, the practitioner occludes (blocks) the vas deferens. This may involve severing, tying, or cauterizing the tubes, or applying metal clips. The procedure lasts approximately thirty minutes.

A no-scalpel vasectomy, or "microvasectomy," is done without incisions. After applying local anesthesia, a doctor clamps the tubes and makes a small puncture in the skin. The tubes are cut and blocked with the same procedures as in a conventional vasectomy. This procedure lasts approximately twenty minutes. The no-scalpel procedure can ease a man's fear about surgery on his genitals and may reduce bleeding and the possibility of infection, bruising, or other complications.[2]

Effectiveness

Male sterilization is highly effective. With correct use (i.e., when the surgery is successful and the couple waits for two "zero" sperm counts), less than one out of one hundred couples will become pregnant in one year. When you add people who use the method incorrectly ("typical use"), still less than one out of one hundred couples will become pregnant.[3]

Though rare, couples become pregnant after a vasectomy for several reasons. First, if a couple has intercourse before all sperm have left the body, pregnancy may result. This occurs if a couple does not use another contraceptive method until two sperm counts show an absence of sperm. This is "user failure," not a failure of the vasectomy itself. A second reason for failure is recanalization of the tubes. During the healing process, white blood cells and other cells can form a "bridge" that can connect the severed ends of the tubes. Viable sperm can then cross the bridge and enter the seminal fluid. Recanalization may be detected in the sperm count tests that follow a vasectomy because it normally occurs within four months of the vasectomy. A third reason for failure is surgical error involving occlusion of the wrong structure or, very rarely, a congenital duplication of the tubes that the surgeon did not notice. These errors occur in approximately four out of one thousand vasectomies.[4] These failures are quite rare, but couples should know that even surgical sterilization carries a failure rate.

181

How to Maximize Effectiveness

Acknowledge fears or questions. An important way to avoid undue stress, regret, and even physical pain is to discuss your fears and questions with your spouse, friends, or doctor. Understanding the vasectomy procedure and its contraceptive mechanism can allay fears about diminished sexuality or masculinity. If you have doubts about being permanently sterile, discuss those thoughts openly and perhaps consider another method.

Follow your doctor's directions. A man remains fertile for some time after a vasectomy because some sperm were present in the vas deferens before the procedure. A doctor will tell you how long to use another method of birth control, usually around two months. In addition, the surgery itself involves self-care including rest and hygienic practices. Follow-up care involves periodic sperm counts that ensure the procedure was successful. When two sperm counts show that the vasectomy was successful, no further follow-up visits are necessary. It usually takes fifteen to twenty ejaculations to expel all sperm.[5]

Monitor your health. If you experience pain, fever, blood, pus, or swelling at the operation site, or any other problems, see a doctor.

Advantages

Permanent. After a vasectomy, a couple need not worry about birth control.

Minimal medical side effects. While there are risks associated with vasectomies, they are not life threatening and are relatively rare. Recovery from the procedure is fairly quick.

Gives primary responsibility to the man. For some men, the ability to shoulder the responsibility for contraception is perceived as an advantage. Removing contraceptive responsibility from the woman is also sometimes perceived as an advantage.

Does not interrupt intercourse. Sterilization allows love-making to happen without any interference from contraceptive devices.

Disadvantages

Unpleasant side effects from the surgery. A man may experience bruises, swelling, or tenderness after surgery. These usually heal by themselves and do not require additional treatment. A doctor may recommend hot or cold packs or extra rest. A small lump, called a granuloma, may appear near the site of the operation. This is caused by sperm leaking from the tubes. These lumps are usually painless and heal by themselves. If a granuloma persists and causes pain, it may require surgical treatment. Granulomas develop in approximately eighteen out of one hundred cases.[6] Surgery may also result in infection, which occurs in approximately seven out of one hundred cases. Treatment with antibiotics is usually successful.

Regret. Some men who choose vasectomy later regret it. Depending upon a man's psychological health, regret may lead to depression, guilt, lowered self-esteem, or loss of masculinity. Some men lose sexual desire or experience erectile dysfunction. Researchers believe these rare cases are not caused by the physical effects of a vasectomy but by emotional stresses.

Potentially serious long-term effects. Researchers have not reached solid conclusions regarding serious health risks associated with vasectomies. Some have suggested a correlation between vasectomy and risk of prostate cancer. In 1993 the National Institutes of Health reviewed medical literature and concluded that research should continue in this area, but medical providers should continue to perform vasectomies and not reverse them to prevent prostate cancer.[7] The second major area of concern is correlation between vasectomy and atherosclerosis (hardening of arteries), which may be linked to sperm antibodies that some men develop following vasectomy. Several research projects on monkeys seemed to show a significant correlation, but research in men has not confirmed these results.[8]

Reversal is difficult and expensive. Vasectomies are only sometimes reversible and involve considerable expense.

Female Sterilization

Mechanism of Action

Female sterilization occludes, or blocks, the fallopian tubes, disrupting the egg's usual travel route. Normally, a mature egg bursts from the ovary and moves through the fallopian tubes, which is where fertilization occurs. When a woman is sterilized, the egg cannot meet sperm in the fallopian tubes. Eggs are still produced in the ovaries, so normal hormonal cycles continue. Like other cells, eggs are reabsorbed by the body when their life-span has expired.

A woman may be sterilized at various times: after a vaginal delivery, after a Caesarean section delivery, after an abortion, or at any time when she is not pregnant. At least half of all sterilizations occur in the immediate postpartum period (within forty-eight hours of delivery). This is because of convenience, ease of surgery, and lowered costs. If a woman is already in the hospital for a birth, sterilization will not require an extended hospital stay.

Female sterilization leaves all female reproductive organs intact; it does not remove the ovaries, uterus, or fallopian tubes. A sterilized woman will continue to menstruate and will eventually experience menopause without disruption due to sterilization. Sterilization does not affect a woman's sexual desire or pleasure. It does not affect feminine characteristics such as voice, facial hair, muscle tone, or breast size.

Types of Female Sterilization

Sterilization procedures can occur through the abdomen (most common) or the vagina. Vaginal procedures are used with increasing rarity in the United States. The most commonly used abdominal procedures are laparoscopy and minilaparotomy. Both require anesthesia, either local (when the woman remains awake for the operation) or general (when the woman sleeps during the operation). Both involve accessing the fallopian tubes and blocking them. Blocking techniques include tying and cutting (liga-

184

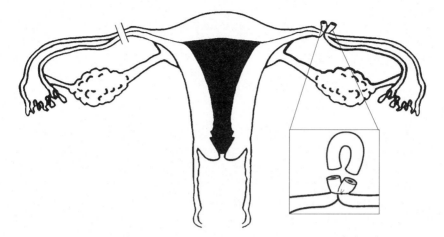

Fig. 16.2. Tubal ligation involves blocking or clipping the fallopian tubes.

tion), sealing (electrocoagulation), or applying clips, clamps, or rings. Sometimes a small piece of tube is removed.[9]

The laparoscopy approach involves making a small incision high in the stomach and inserting an instrument (a laparoscope) that allows the surgeon to see the tubes. A second incision, or puncture, is made just above the pubic area, where instruments are inserted to access and occlude the tubes. The minilaparotomy approach involves one incision just above the pubic area. By manually manipulating the uterus, the surgeon moves the tubes into the incision site and blocks them. It is possible to access the tubes through the vagina, but this approach is surgically difficult and can introduce infection into the vagina or cervix. It is used in exceptional circumstances.

The FDA approved a nonsurgical procedure for female sterilization in 2002. Named Essure, it involves inserting a tiny spring into each fallopian tube. The device irritates the tube's lining to cause scar tissue to grow. After three months, the scar tissue blocks the tubes entirely. This procedure involves local anesthetic, and may be done in a gynecologist's office. Unlike surgical tubal ligation, a woman must use other birth control for several months after the Essure procedure.

185

A hysterectomy, removal of the uterus, has a contraceptive effect but is not performed for contraceptive purposes alone. Your medical provider can help you decide which method would be best for you.[10]

Effectiveness

Female sterilization is highly effective, with both typical- and perfect-use rates measured at .5 percent. This means that in the year following sterilization, less than one out of one hundred women will become pregnant.

Though rare, women become pregnant after sterilization for several reasons. If a woman was pregnant at the time of sterilization, the pregnancy can continue successfully. A second reason for unintended pregnancy is failure of the occlusion method. As with the vas deferens, the fallopian tubes can spontaneously reattach, allowing for movement of the egg through the tubes. This happens rarely but is more likely to happen when the tubes are occluded with clips. A third reason is surgical error. Leading researchers estimate that surgical error accounts for 30 to 50 percent of female sterilization failures. A surgeon may incorrectly identify the tubes or improperly occlude the tubes. A final reason for failure is flaws in surgical equipment or occlusion devices. These reasons for failure are serious, but even when combined, they result in unintended pregnancies for only five out of one thousand women.[11]

How to Maximize Effectiveness

Choose an experienced surgeon. Surgeons who perform fewer than one hundred sterilizations per year have a much higher complication rate than more experienced surgeons.[12] Don't be shy about asking a doctor or surgeon what her or his experience level is.

Follow your doctor's protocol. Listen carefully to what your medical provider says, and write it down if necessary. Follow instructions for postsurgery self-care, including rest and hygienic practices.

186

Be attentive to your health. See a doctor if after sterilization you experience fever, dizziness, fainting, abdominal pain, bleeding, or fluid from the incision.

Advantages

Permanent. After tubal ligation a couple need not worry about birth control.

Allows female control. For some women, definitively ending their ability to have additional children is perceived as an advantage.

Does not interrupt intercourse. Sterilization allows love-making to happen without any interference from contraceptive devices.

Disadvantages

Unpleasant side effects from surgery. Complications occur in less than one percent of all sterilization procedures. Possible complications include problems associated with anesthesia, excess bleeding or hemorrhage, and infection. It is also possible to damage a nearby organ such as the bowels or uterus. Choosing an experienced surgeon and monitoring your own health after the procedure will help reduce this small risk.

Regret. Some women who choose tubal ligation regret it later. Be sure that you are confident of your decision. Other than regret, sterilized women do not experience any more psychological problems than do nonsterilized women.[13]

Probability of ectopic (tubal) pregnancy if method fails. A major study that included 10,685 women concluded that 7.5 out of 1,000 sterilized women will experience an ectopic pregnancy within ten years of sterilization.[14] An ectopic pregnancy is an "out of place" pregnancy in which the fertilized egg implants in the fallopian tube and begins growing. Many ectopic pregnancies terminate naturally, but if it continues, it is extremely dangerous for the woman's health. If a pregnancy is ectopic, it is not viable and cannot continue to term. Nonsterilized women experience ectopic pregnancies at a rate of .5 percent to 1 percent.

Menstrual disturbance. Research on menstrual changes caused by sterilization is active, varied, and controversial. Post–tubal ligation syndrome refers to symptoms including painful menstruation, heavy bleeding, and changes in cycle length and regularity. Leading researchers believe that a connection between sterilization and post–tubal ligation syndrome is unsubstantiated.[15] They also believe that most instances of menstrual changes are due to the stoppage of prior use of birth control pills or IUDs. Ongoing research is necessary, however, and is under way.

Death. Statistics from 1980 suggest that in the United States between one and two women out of one hundred thousand die from sterilization procedures.[16] In developing countries, about five women per one hundred thousand die.[17] While this is a serious risk, pregnancy is riskier. Maternal mortality in the United States is measured at approximately 7.9 deaths per one hundred thousand live births.[18]

Cost

At a public clinic, a vasectomy may cost from $250 to $400. At a private clinic, it may cost from $500 to $1000. Female sterilization may cost around $2,500 at a private clinic and $1,200 at a public clinic.[19]

Questions for Conversation

1. What are your reasons for considering permanent birth control? As a couple, are your reasons compatible or significantly different?

2. Consider the rest of your life without children or without additional children. Is that a good scenario? Might you later desire children?

3. What for you is most appealing about sterilization? How does your spouse view this method's advantages?

4. What for you is sterilization's most important drawback? How does your spouse view the disadvantages?

5. Are the disadvantages and medical side effects of sterilization acceptable to you?

6. Sterilization prevents pregnancy by altering a man or woman's anatomy to prevent sperm and egg from meeting. For you, is this an ethically acceptable mechanism of action? Why or why not?

7. Will this method allow you to better express and enjoy sexual intimacy? Might it suppress sexual intimacy? Why?

8. Discuss any fears or hesitations you may have about vasectomies. Might it affect the man's sense of masculinity? Might it affect your sex life, for better or for worse?

9. Discuss any fears or hesitations you may have about female sterilization. Might it affect the woman's sense of femininity? Might it affect your sex life, for better or for worse?

10. On a scale of one to ten (one meaning "absolutely not" and ten meaning "this looks really good"), how do you rank this method? How does your spouse rank it?

11. As a couple, do you assess sterilization in a similar way or in different ways? Are any of your disagreements significant enough to warrant consideration of a different method?

Epilogue

Not long ago I facilitated a public dialogue about dating and boundaries with Christian college students. Students articulated various and mutually exclusive viewpoints they had heard from Christian leaders. I expected the discussion topic to be, "Which point of view is morally correct?" Students didn't raise this question; rather, they began to speak their own minds in light of their experiences. One student said, "Given my sexual past, I've chosen not to even kiss my boyfriend. It's better for me to be extreme about sexual boundaries, because I've crossed all the boundaries in the past." Another said, "For me, kissing and holding hands with my boyfriend is a good way of expressing care. We talk about boundaries, and I talk with my female friends about my dating relationships as a form of accountability." Another said, "I've never had a date! I just listen, take it all in, and I'll take my own stance when the time comes."

These young adults are making their own way through dating, sex, and intimacy, sorting through conflicting advice they receive from friends, family, Christian leaders, and secular media. I was impressed with their eagerness to take responsibility for their own lives rather than walk lockstep in the path prescribed by a person in authority. They talked and listened to each other, exploring options, discarding some ideas, and creating some new possibilities. They questioned, "What sort of framework might help us each make wise choices in our lives?" We talked about the way God made sex, friendship, bodies, and marriage, and how biblical themes like stewardship, love, and faithfulness might guide our intimate decisions.

Likewise in matters of contraception, I don't claim to speak for God or to pronounce the right choice for every Christian. My biases are strong: I value birth control that treats fertility as a gift to be stewarded, not a disease to be medicated away. I value simplicity, natural approaches to health care, and self-knowledge, and these values guide many of my life choices, including contraception. My husband and I have found freedom in taking up the responsibility of defining and living out our values together, in the company of our Christian community. We want our decisions to be well informed, reflective, and fully ours. Perhaps I shouldn't have been so impressed or surprised by the college students' desire to do the same.

Doing the right thing is partly about the choices we make, but it's also about the way we make choices. Steve, a twenty-two-year-old man who read a draft of this book, said, "My fiancée and I have so much to talk about. We are pretty sure we want to use the pill, but we really need to consider ethics, side effects, and other options. We want to make the best choice we can make." He and his fiancée were learning to talk about sex with frankness and honesty so they could have a better marriage and make wise choices even in the most intimate parts of life.

Carla, a twenty-one-year-old married woman, had made a contraceptive choice with limited information and felt trapped. "I've been dissatisfied with my birth control choice ever since I got married, but I didn't know what else to do. I'm going to learn more about some other options and get moving toward making a change." Knowledge about fertility helped her take more control and responsibility for her life and helped her broach the subject with her husband.

Andy, an eighteen-year-old man, said in a manuscript discussion group, "I loved the chapter on fertility and anatomy. I don't even have a girlfriend, but if I ever date someone, I'll be the best boyfriend ever!" Indeed, Andy will make a great boyfriend for some lucky woman because his knowledge will help him be a better friend to a woman, even if his contraceptive choices are still in the future.

Medical information changes and new contraceptive methods come on the market frequently. I hope, therefore, that this book will facilitate the development of your own framework for thinking about sexuality and fertility. And I hope you'll be able to use this framework to learn about contraceptive options and make good decisions. The model of *shalom* is one I learned and adapted from wise teachers in my life, and I pass it along to you. Doing that which results in peace—with God, each other, self, and the world—can help you make wise choices in all of life, even in the area of birth control.

Appendix

Effectiveness Table of All Contraceptive Methods

When a couple uses birth control, they want to know how well it will work. Some couples want extremely high effectiveness, while others are satisfied with a more moderate rate. On the one hand, all modern contraceptive methods are highly effective. Some are more effective than others, but all provide substantial protection against pregnancy when compared to using no birth control. On the other hand, no modern contraceptive provides absolute protection against pregnancy (though sterilization comes very close). The risk of pregnancy is always present in sexual relationships, and couples must make choices about how to manage that risk.

Measuring the effectiveness of contraceptives is extremely complex and results are contested among researchers. Scholars use different kinds of studies, statistical analyses, and reports to develop and share their work. The leading scholars in the field of contraception have developed the statistics used in this book. They are summarized in the chart on pages 196–97.

I give two numbers for each method, though I realize it can be difficult to understand what the numbers mean. One number refers to correct-use efficacy. This refers to the percent

Percent of Women Experiencing an Unintended Pregnancy in the First Year of Typical or Perfect Use

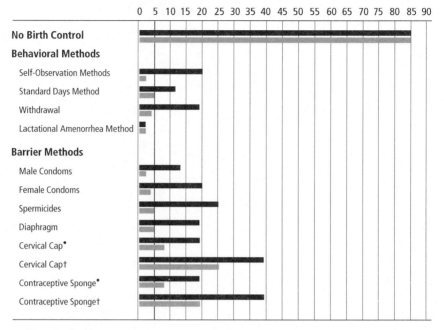

■   Typical Use
▨   Perfect Use
•   For a woman who has not had a baby
†   For a woman who has had at least one baby
NA   Not available

Sources: Effectiveness rates for all methods except lactational amenorrhea and the standard days method are from Robert Hatcher et al., *Contraceptive Technology,* 17th ed. (New York: Arden Media, 1998). For lactational amenorrhea, John Guillebaud, *Contraception: Your Questions Answered* (London: Churchill Livingstone, 1999), 37. For standard days method, Marcos Arevalo, Victoria Jennings, and Irit Sinai, "Efficacy of a new Method of Family Planning: The Standard Days Methods," *Contraception* 65 (May 2002): 333–38.

of people *who use the method correctly* and experience an unintended pregnancy within the first year of use. The second number refers to typical-use efficacy. This refers to the percent of people *who sometimes use the method incorrectly* and experience an unintended pregnancy within the first year of use.

196

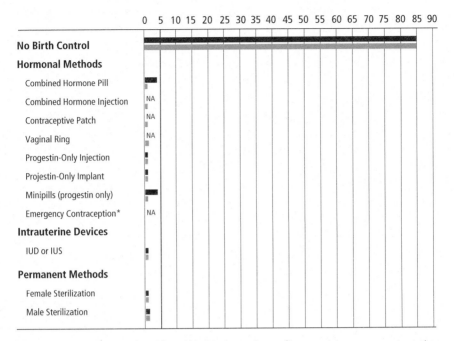

	0	5	10	15	20	25	30	35	40	45	50	55	60	65	70	75	80	85	90

No Birth Control

Hormonal Methods

Combined Hormone Pill

Combined Hormone Injection — NA

Contraceptive Patch — NA

Vaginal Ring — NA

Progestin-Only Injection

Projestin-Only Implant

Minipills (progestin only)

Emergency Contraception* — NA

Intrauterine Devices

IUD or IUS

Permanent Methods

Female Sterilization

Male Sterilization

*Emergency contraception. When taken within seventy-two hours of intercourse, emergency contraception reduces the risk of pregnancy by at least 75 percent. Because emergency contraception is not used regularly, its effectiveness rates are different than the others on the chart.

Let's take the male condom as an example. The male condom has a 97 percent correct-use effectiveness rate. If one hundred couples use a male condom consistently and correctly for one year, about three couples will become pregnant. These pregnancies are due to faults in the method itself; for condoms, this means a condom broke, slipped, or had flaws that allowed sperm to pass through. A 97 percent effectiveness rate *does not* mean that a condom will fail three times out of every one hundred uses.

The male condom has an 86 percent typical-use effectiveness rate. This means that if one hundred couples make typical use of a male condom for a year, about fourteen will become pregnant. These pregnancies are due to the behaviors of users, not defects

197

or failures in the method itself. Typical use of a condom could include using a condom incorrectly or using it only occasionally.

These statistics show that two main factors determine the effectiveness of a contraceptive: the inherent effectiveness of the method and the behavior of the user or users. People often focus exclusively on the inherent effectiveness of the method. For methods such as the IUD, implants, or sterilization, user behavior has a low to moderate influence on effectiveness. For other methods, such as self-observation methods, vaginal barriers, or most hormonal contraceptives, user behavior greatly influences the effectiveness of the method. Obviously, these methods work only when used properly and consistently. In addition, frequency of intercourse and age (fertility declines with age) influence the effectiveness of a contraceptive.

When assessing the effectiveness of a method, it's important to consider both the method itself and your own use of the method.

Notes

Introduction

1. Boston Women's Health Collective, *The New Our Bodies, Ourselves: Updated and Expanded for the '90s* (New York: Simon & Schuster, 1992), 239.

2. Pope Paul VI, *Humanae Vitae*, reprinted in *On Moral Medicine: Theological Perspectives in Medical Ethics*, ed. Stephen Lammers and Allan Verhey, 2d ed. (Grand Rapids: Eerdmans, 1998), 434–38.

3. Robyn Minahan and I surveyed sixty couples and interviewed eight about their contraceptive choices. I also gathered data from informal interviews, fertility awareness courses, and on-line chats.

4. Jon Knowles and Marcia Ringel, *All about Birth Control: A Complete Guide* (New York: Random House, 1998), ix. Others include Vern Bullough and Bonnie Bullough, *Contraception: A Guide to Birth Control Methods*, 2d ed. (Amherst, N.Y.: Prometheus, 1997); Beverly Winikoff and Suzanne Wymelenberg, *The Whole Truth about Contraception: A Guide to Safe and Effective Choices* (Washington, D.C.: Joseph Henry, 1997).

5. Helpful technical texts include John Guillebaud, *Contraception: Your Questions Answered* (London: Churchill Livingstone, 1999); Robert Hatcher et al., *Contraceptive Technology*, 17th ed. (New York: Irvington, 1998).

6. Nash Herndon, "Men Influence Contraceptive Use," *Network* 18, no. 3 (1998), http://www.fhi.org/en/fp/fppubs/network/v18%2D3/index.html.

7. Isaiah Ndong and William Finger, "Introduction: Male Responsibility for Reproductive Health," *Network* 18, no. 3 (1998), http:// www. fhi.org/en/fp/fppubs/network/v18%2D3/nt1831.html.

NOTES

Chapter 1 *Birth Control*

1. Interested readers may find valuable presentations of pro- and anticontraception positions in Stephen Lammers and Allan Verhey, eds., *On Moral Medicine: Theological Perspectives in Medical Ethics*, 2d ed. (Grand Rapids: Eerdmans, 1998); "Contraception: A Symposium," *First Things* 88 (December 1998): 17–29. For a concise defense of Catholic doctrine, see John F. Kippley, *Birth Control and Christian Discipleship*, 2d ed. (Cincinnati: Couple to Couple League, 1994).

2. Janet Farrell Brodie, *Contraception and Abortion in Nineteenth-Century America* (Ithaca: Cornell University, 1994); Angus McLaren, *A History of Contraception: From Antiquity to the Present Day* (Padstow, England: T. J. Press, 1990).

3. The American definition of "obscene" closely followed British legal precedents. In 1868 Lord Chief Justice Cockburn of England wrote, "The test of obscenity is this, whether the tendency of the matter charged as obscenity is to deprave and corrupt those whose minds are open to such immoral influences, and into whose hands a publication of this sort may fall." Alvah Sulloway, *Birth Control and Catholic Doctrine* (Boston: Beacon, 1959), 12.

4. Ibid., 16.

5. C. Paul Hodgkinson, "Birth Control," in *Religion and Birth Control: Twenty-One Medical Specialists Write in Plain Language about Control of Conception, Therapeutic Abortion, Sterilization, Natural Childbirth, Artificial Insemination*, ed. John Clover Monsma (Garden City, N.Y.: Doubleday, 1963), 3.

6. Sulloway, *Birth Control and Catholic Doctrine*, 20.

7. Alan Wilkinson, "Three Sexual Issues," *Theology* 91 (March 1988): 18.

8. 1920 Lambeth Conference of Anglican Bishops: Resolution 68, http://www.anglicancommunion.org/acns/archive/1920/1920-69.htm.

9. 1920 Lambeth Conference of Anglican Bishops: Resolution 70, http://www.anglicancommunion.org/acns/archive/1920/1920-70.htm.

10. The abolition of Comstock laws allowed for contraceptive information dissemination but did not require it. Many medical schools and doctors did not address contraception until the 1940s. Two Supreme Court cases resolved access issues. *Griswold v. Connecticut* (1965) declared anticontraceptive legislation unconstitutional, requiring doctors to supply married couples with contraceptive information. Seven years later *Eisenstadt v. Baird* (1972) extended that right to unmarried individuals.

11. 1930 Lambeth Conference of Anglican Bishops: Resolution 15, http://www.anglicancommunion.org/acns/archive/1930/1930-15.htm. For later development, see Susannah Coolidge, "Chastity in a World of Three Billion Souls," *Anglican Theological Review* 37 (1955): 41–49.

12. Wilkinson, "Three Sexual Issues," 130.

13. Kippley, *Birth Control and Christian Discipleship*, 5. See also Morris Fishbein, *The Medical Follies* (New York: Boni & Liveright, 1925); Paul King Jewett, "A Case for Birth Control," *Christian Century* 21 (24 May 1961): 651–52; Monsma, ed., *Religion and Birth Control*; William Robinson, *Birth Control, or The*

Limitation of Offspring Prevention (New York: Eugenics Publishing, 1926); and M. O. Vincent, "A Christian View of Contraception," *Christianity Today* 8, no. 3 (1968): 14–15.

14. Sulloway, *Birth Control and Catholic Doctrine*, 41.

15. Ibid., 43.

16. Kippley, *Birth Control and Christian Discipleship*, 9.

17. John D'Emilio and Estelle Freedman, *Intimate Matters: A History of Sexuality in America*, 2d ed. (Chicago: University of Chicago, 1997), 256.

18. Helen Gurley Brown, *Sex and the Single Girl: The Unmarried Woman's Guide to Men* (New York: Pocket Books, 1962), 212.

19. Pope Paul VI, *Humanae Vitae*, reprinted in *On Moral Medicine*, 437.

20. J. Budziszewski, in "Contraception: A Symposium," 17–29.

21. Charles Curran, "The Contraceptive Revolution and the Human Condition," *American Journal of Theology and Philosophy* 3 (May 1982): 59.

22. Thomas Shapiro, *Population Control Politics: Women, Sterilization, and Reproductive Choice* (Philadelphia: Temple University, 1985).

23. Leo Marx, "Does Improved Technology Mean Progress?" in *Technology and the Future*, ed. Albert Teich, 7th ed. (New York: St. Martin's, 1997), 3–14.

24. Curran, "The Contraceptive Revolution," 42.

25. Ibid., 59.

Chapter 2 *Making Wise Choices about Birth Control*

1. Charles Chaput, in "Contraception: A Symposium," *First Things* 88 (December 1998): 17–29; Monica Bahati Kuumba, "Perpetuating Neo-Colonialism through Population Control: South Africa and the United States," *Africa Today* 40, no. 3 (1993): 79–86; Angus McLaren, *A History of Contraception: From Antiquity to the Present Day* (Padstow, England: T. J. Press, 1990); and Dorothy Roberts, "Black Women and the Pill," *Family Planning Perspectives* 32, no. 2 (2000): 92–93.

2. John Guillebaud, *Contraception: Your Questions Answered* (London: Churchill Livingstone, 1999), 463.

3. Barbara Barnett, "First Time Users Have Diverse Needs," *Network* 19, no. 4 (1999), http://www.fhi.org/en/fp/fppubs/network/v19%2D4/nt1941.html.

4. United Nations, *The World's Women 2000: Trends and Statistics* (report, New York, 2000), 33.

5. Barnett, "First Time Users Have Diverse Needs."

6. Joan Marie Kraft and James E. Coverdill, "Employment and the Use of Birth Control by Sexually Active Single Hispanic, Black, and White Women," *Demography* 31, no. 45 (1994): 593–603; Jennifer Malat, "Racial Differences in Norplant Use in the United States," *Social Science and Medicine* 40 (May 2000): 1297–1309; Roberts, "Black Women and the Pill."

7. This survey included 235 women ages eighteen to forty-nine. Pharmacia & Upjohn, "'What Women Want' Global Survey," 2000, http://www.birth controlresources.com.

8. Roy Branson, "The Secularization of American Medicine," in *On Moral Medicine: Theological Perspectives in Medical Ethics*, ed. Stephen Lammers and Allan Verhey, 2d ed. (Grand Rapids: Eerdmans, 1998), 13.

9. M. Marshall, V. Jennings, and J. Cachan, "Reproductive Health Awareness: An Integrated Approach to Obtaining a High Quality of Health," *Advances in Contraception* 13 (1997): 313.

Chapter 3 *The Birds, the Bees, and the Beginning of Life*

1. Julia Weeks Simanski, "The Birds and the Bees: An Analysis of Advice Given to Parents through Popular Press," *Adolescence* 33 (1998): 33–46.

2. Barbara Barnett, "Fertility Awareness Benefits Couples," *Network* 17, no. 1 (1996), http://www.fhi.org/en/fp/fppubs/network/v17-1/nt1711.html. See also Barbara Barnett, "Fertility Awareness Affects Method Use," *Network* 17, no. 1 (1996), http://www.fhi.org/en/fp/fppubs/network/v17%2D1/nt1713.html.

3. Helpful sources include Barbara Kass-Annese and Hal C. Danzer, *The Fertility Awareness Handbook: The Natural Guide to Avoiding or Achieving Pregnancy*, 2d ed. (Alameda, Calif.: Hunter House, 1992); Toni Weschler, *Taking Charge of Your Fertility: The Definitive Guide to Natural Birth Control and Pregnancy Achievement*, rev. ed. (New York: Harper Perennial, 2001).

4. *The Guinness Book of Records 1995* (New York: Guinness, 1994).

5. S. Guha et al., "Phase II Trial of a Vas Deferens Injectable Contraceptive for the Male," *Contraception* 56 (October 1997): 245–50; Judith Richter, *Vaccination against Pregnancy: Miracle or Menace?* (New Jersey: Zed, 1996); G. Shetty et al., "Use of Norethisterone and Estradiol in Mini Doses as a Contraceptive in the Male," *Contraception* 56 (Oct. 1997): 257–65.

6. George Maloof, "Psychophysiological Aspects of Fertility," *International Review of Natural Family Planning* 2, no. 2 (1978): 161–84.

Chapter 4 *Don't Try This at Home*

1. Philip Williams, "Modern Contraceptives: Their Values and Limitations," *Human Fertility* 5 (1950): 1, 10–15.

2. For a thorough history of herbal contraceptives, see Burkhard Bilger, *Eve's Herbs: A History of Contraception and Abortion in the West* (Cambridge: Harvard University Press, 1997).

3. Sister Zeus, *HomeSpun: A Women's Networking Newsletter*, http://www.sis terzeus.com.

Chapter 5 *Self-Observation Methods*

1. The cervix changes in response to hormones. When a woman is infertile, the cervix is low, hard, dry, and closed. When she is fertile, the cervix is high, wet, soft, and open. A woman can monitor these changes by reaching one or two fingers into the vagina to touch the cervix. This symptom is reliable but is usually considered an optional or back-up method to cervical fluid and waking temperature.

2. A. R. Martinez, "Prediction and Detection of the Fertile Phase of the Menstrual Cycle," *Advances in Contraception* 13 (1997): 131–38.

3. Persona is the most widely marketed fertility monitor and is available in Britain and on the Internet. See http://www.persona.org.uk. Two websites that link to fertility monitor information are http://www.birthcontrol.com/ and that of Global Health Options, http://www.g-h-o.co.uk.

4. The "calendar" and "rhythm" methods are the same and refer to a calendar-based method of determining fertile times. Using a calendar, a woman predicts the beginning of her next period and counts back a certain number of days. She considers several days before and after that midpoint to be fertile. This method is more effective than no contraception but is not nearly as effective as NFP or FAM because it makes guesses about fertile times. Most women do not have perfectly regular cycles, and even women with regular cycles may experience occasional irregularity due to stress, illness, or other factors. NFP and FAM are based on daily observation of fertility and involve no guesswork about the length of cycles or the length of fertile times.

5. Victoria H. Jennings, Virginia M. Lamprecht, and Deborah Kowal, "Fertility Awareness Methods," in Robert Hatcher et al., *Contraceptive Technology*, 17th ed. (New York: Irvington, 1998); V. Lamprecht and J. Trussell, "Natural Family Planning Effectiveness: Evaluating Published Reports," *Advances in Contraception* 13 (1997): 155–65.

6. Jennings et al., "Fertility Awareness Methods," 323.

7. P. Frank-Herrmann et al., "Natural Family Planning with and without Barrier Method Use in the Fertile Phase: Efficacy in Relation to Sexual Behavior: A German Prospective Long-Term Study," *Advances in Contraception* 13 (1997): 79–189.

8. Toni Weschler, *Taking Charge of Your Fertility: The Definitive Guide to Natural Birth Control and Pregnancy Achievement*, rev. ed. (New York: HarperCollins, 2001); Merryl Winstein, *Your Fertility Signs: Using Them to Achieve or Avoid Pregnancy, Naturally* (St. Louis: Smooth Stone, 1999).

9. J. Bonnar, V. Lamprecht, and E. O'Conner, "Alternatives to Vaginal Intercourse Practiced During the Fertile Time Among Calendar Users in Ireland," *Advances in Contraception* 13 (1997): 173–77.

10. Karen Berhow, "Natural Family Planning Has Blessed Our Marriage," *The Catholic Spirit* (6 August 1998): 13; M. France, J. France, and K. Townend, "Natural Family Planning in New Zealand: A Study of Continuation Rates and Characteristics of Users," *Advances in Contraception* 13 (1997):

191–98; Virginia Lamprecht and Cecilia Pyper, "Opinion: Fertility Awareness and Natural Family Planning," *Network* 17, no. 1 (1996), http:// www. fhi.org/en/fp/fppubs/network/v17%2D1/nt17111.html.

11. The Creighton Model NaProEducation Technology is a new approach to teaching the ovulation method and requires approximately nine teaching and follow-up sessions over the course of a year. Initial studies show high effectiveness rates associated with this approach. Thomas Hilgers and Joseph Stanford, "Creighton Model NaProEducation Technology for Avoiding Pregnancy," *The Journal of Reproductive Medicine* 43, no. 6 (1998): 495–502.

Chapter 6 *Standard Days Method*

1. Marcos Arevalo, Irit Sinai, and Victoria Jennings, "A Fixed Formula to Define the Fertile Window of the Menstrual Cycle as the Basis of a Simple Method of Natural Family Planning," *Contraception* 60 (1999): 357–60.

2. More information about SDM and about purchasing CycleBeads may be found at http://www.cyclebeads.com.

3. Institute for Reproductive Health, "Standard Days Method: A Modern, Effective Method of Family Planning," *The Awareness Project Research Update*, May 2002, http://www.irh.org/ru-sdm-modern.htm.

4. Karen Springen, "Family Jewels," *Newsweek*, 10 June 2002, 8; "New Natural Method of Family Planning over 95 Percent Effective in Preventing Pregnancy, Study Finds," *Georgetown News*, 10 June 2002.

5. The effectiveness study involved 478 women in Bolivia, Peru, and the Philippines. Marcos Arevalo, Victoria Jennings, and Irit Sinai, "Efficacy of a New Method of Family Planning: The Standard Days Method," *Contraception* 65, no. 5 (2002): 333–38.

Chapter 7 *Withdrawal*

1. Withdrawal is used around the world, most often in Romania, Turkey, the former Czech Republic, Sri Lanka, Mauritius, Brazil, Colombia, the Philippines, Trinidad and Tobago, and Zimbabwe. Researchers have not collected excellent data regarding withdrawal's effectiveness. This is because many people do not report it as a method used and because many use withdrawal only occasionally. Large-scale studies of couples that use withdrawal correctly and consistently for months at a time have not been possible. William R. Finger, "Contraceptive Update: Withdrawal Popular in Some Cultures," *Network* 17, no. 1 (1996), http://www.fhi.org/en/fp/fppubs/network/v17%2D1/nt1717 .html. Deborah Kowal, "Coitus Interruptus (Withdrawal)," in Robert Hatcher et al., *Contraceptive Technology*, 17th ed. (New York: Irvington, 1998), 304.

2. Scientific controversy surrounds the issue of whether or not sperm are present in pre-ejaculate. The prior consensus was that sperm were present in pre-ejaculate, but new studies show few or no sperm (though these studies

used small numbers of men). G. Ilaria et al., "Detection of HIV-1 DNA sequences in Pre-Ejaculatory Fluid," *Lancet* 340 (1992): 1469; J. Pudney et al., "Pre-ejaculatory Fluid as Potential Vector for Sexual Transmission of HIV-1," *Lancet* 340 (1992): 1470.

3. Cynthia Myntti et al., "Challenging the Stereotypes: Men, Withdrawal, and Reproductive Health in Lebanon," *Contraception* 65, no. 2 (2002): 165–70.

4. George Arthur Buttrick, ed., *The Interpreter's Bible* (New York: Abingdon, 1952); Victor P. Hamilton, *The Book of Genesis Chapters 18–50* (Grand Rapids: Eerdmans, 1995); Derek Kidner, *Genesis: An Introduction and Commentary* (Downers Grove, Ill.: InterVarsity, 1967); Catherine Clark Kroeger and Mary J. Evans, eds., *The IVP Women's Bible Commentary* (Downers Grove, Ill.: InterVarsity, 2000); Gordon J. Wenham, *Word Biblical Commentary: Genesis 16–50*, vol. 2 (Dallas: Word, 1994).

Chapter 8 *Lactational Amenorrhea Method*

1. Kathy I. Kennedy and James Trussell, "Postpartum Contraception and Lactation," in Robert Hatcher et al., *Contraceptive Technology*, 17th ed. (New York: Irvington, 1998), 589–614.

2. Barbara Kass-Annese and Hal C. Danzer, *The Fertility Awareness Handbook: The Natural Guide to Avoiding or Achieving Pregnancy*, 2d ed. (Alameda, Calif.: Hunter House, 1992), 116.

3. K. Kennedy, R. Rivera, and A. McNeilly, "Consensus Statement on the Use of Breastfeeding as a Family Planning Method," *Contraception* 39 (1989): 477–96; John Guillebaud, *Contraception: Your Questions Answered* (London: Churchill Livingstone, 1999), 37.

4. M. Labbok, K. Cooney, and S. Coly, *Guidelines for Breastfeeding and the Lactational Amenorrhea Method*, 3d ed. (Institute for Reproductive Health, Washington, D.C., pamphlet, 1994).

5. In a study of LAM users in the United States, women said they liked LAM because it was natural, had no side effects, and is easy and convenient. Virginia Hight-Laukaran et al., "Multicenter Study of the Lactational Amenorrhea Method (LAM): II. Acceptability, Utility, and Policy Implications," *Contraception* 55 (1997): 337–46.

6. Collaborative Group on Hormonal Factors in Breast Cancer, "Breast Cancer and Breastfeeding: Collaborative Reanalysis of Individual Data from 47 Epidemiological Studies in 30 Countries, Including 50,302 Women with Breast Cancer and 96,973 Women without the Disease," *Lancet* 360 (2002): 187; John F. Kippley and Sheila K. Kippley, *The Art of Natural Family Planning*, 4th ed. (Cincinnati: Couple to Couple League, 1999), 334–39.

Chapter 9 *Condoms*

1. Caroline Gilmore et al., eds., "The Development of Non-Latex Condoms," in *The Latex Condom: Recent Advances, Future Directions* (Research Triangle Park, NC: Family Health International, 1999); David A. Grimes, "Conference Report: Updates from the XVI World Congress of the International Federation of Gynecology and Obstetrics," *Medscape Women's Health* 5 (2000).

2. Gilmore, "The Development of Non-Latex Condoms." Also see G. Farr et al., "Contraceptive Efficacy and Acceptability of the Female Condom," *American Journal of Public Health* 84 (1994): 1960–64.

3. D. Lee Warner and Robert A. Hatcher, "Male Condoms," in Robert Hatcher et al., *Contraceptive Technology*, 17th ed. (New York: Irvington, 1998), 328. This does not mean that three out of every one hundred condoms fail. It means that if one hundred couples use condoms with every act of intercourse for one year (thousands of condoms used), three couples will become pregnant. The failure rate is measured in terms of couples, not in numbers of condoms used.

4. Felicia Stewart, "Vaginal Barriers," in Hatcher et al., *Contraceptive Technology*, 376–77. A more recent study of female condoms among 190 Japanese women showed a typical use failure rate of 3.2 percent, much closer to male condom rates. James Trussell, "Contraceptive Efficacy of the Reality Female Condom," *Contraception* 58 (1998): 148–49.

5. Hatcher et al., *A Pocket Guide to Managing Contraception*, 1999–2000 ed. (Tiger, Ga.: Bridging the Gap Communications), 43. Most couples who use condoms never experience condom failure. Researchers have identified correlations between certain user characteristics and condom failure. The types of people who most often experience condom failure have one or more of the following characteristics: young, not living with one's sexual partner, having multiple sexual partners, low income, and low education. If you have one or more of these characteristics, it does not mean that you, as an individual, cannot use condoms correctly. It does mean, however, that *groups* of people with these characteristics experience condom failure more often than other *groups* of people. Studies that reached these conclusions include L. Linberg, F. Sonenstein, L. Ku, et al., "Young Men's Experience with Condom Breakage," *Family Planning Perspectives* 29 (1997): 128–31; Michael J. Rosenberg and Michael S. Waught, "Latex Condom Breakage and Slippage in a Controlled Clinical Trial," *Contraception* 56 (1997): 17–21; S. Rugpao, C. Beyrer, S. Toanabutra, et al., "Multiple Condom Use and Decreased Condom Breakage and Slippage in Thailand," *Journal of Acquired Immune Deficiency Syndrome and Human Retrovirology* 14 (1997): 169–73; A. Spruyt, M. J. Steiner, C. Joanis, et al., "Identifying Condom Users at Risk of Breakage and Slippage: Three International Sites," *American Journal of Public Health* 88, no. 2 (1998): 239–44.

6. F. J. DiClemente, G. M. Wingood, R. Crosby, et al., "Condom Carrying Is Not Associated with Condom Use and Lower Prevalence of Sexually

Transmitted Diseases Among Minority Adolescent Females," *Sexually Transmitted Diseases* 28 (2001): 444–47.

7. Mark Gabbay and Alan Gibbs, "Does Additional Lubrication Reduce Condom Failure?" *Contraception* 53 (1996): 155–58.

8. In a 2001 report, the National Institutes of Health found that correct and consistent use of male latex condoms reduces transmission of HIV/AIDS in men and women and gonorrhea in men. They said research is insufficient to make strong claims regarding the effectiveness of condoms in preventing the spread of gonorrhea in women or chlamydia, syphilis, chancroid, trichomoniasis, genital herpes, and the human papilloma virus (HPV) in men and women. The panel emphasized that condoms may be effective in preventing these STDs, but more research must be completed in order to make strong claims.

9. Desiree Lie, "Contraception Update for the Primary Care Physician, Conference Summary of the American Academy of Family Physicians, 52d Annual Scientific Assembly," *Family Medicine Summaries*, http://www.medscape.com (2000).

10. Costs for male condoms are from "Condoms Get Better," *Consumer Reports*, June 1999. Costs for female condoms are from on-line retailers.

Chapter 10 *Spermicides*

1. John Guillebaud, *Contraception: Your Questions Answered* (London: Churchill Livingstone, 1999), 84; Willard Cates Jr. and Elizabeth G. Raymond, "Vaginal Spermicides," in Robert Hatcher et al., *Contraceptive Technology*, 17th ed. (New York: Irvington, 1998), 360.

2. People frequently exposed to large doses of N-9 may experience problems related to vaginal absorption of the chemical or liver toxicity (Cates and Raymond, "Vaginal Spermicides," 365). One study of Nairobi prostitutes showed damage to the vagina from frequent exposure to N-9, the most frequently used spermicidal chemical. These women were exposed to the chemical four times a day for fourteen days. This is not likely to be a problem for people who have intercourse fewer than four times a day. Guillebaud, *Contraception: Your Questions Answered*, 86.

3. Barbara Richardson, "Nonoxynol-9 as a Vaginal Microbicide for Prevention of Sexually Transmitted Infections: It's Time to Move On," *Journal of the American Medical Association* 287 (2002): 1171–72; Ronald Roddy et al., "Effect of Nonoxynol-9 Gel on Urogenital Gonorrhea and Chlamydial Infection: A Randomized Controlled Trial," *Journal of the American Medical Association* 287, no. 9 (2002): 1117–22.

4. Hatcher et al., *A Pocket Guide to Managing Contraception*, 1999–2000 ed. (Tiger, Ga.: Bridging the Gap Communications), 57.

Chapter 11 *Vaginal Barriers*

1. For more information about the Lea Contraceptive, see http://www.birth control.com/.

2. For more information about the Oves contraceptive cap, see http://www.birthcontrol.com/.

3. Kim Best, "New Devices May Be Easier to Use," *Network* 29, no. 2 (2000), http://www.fhi.org/en/fp/fppubs/network/v20%2D2/nt2023.html.

4. For purchasing information, see http://www.contraceptivesponges.com/ and http://www.birthcontrol.com/.

5. Felicia Stewart, "Vaginal Barriers," in Hatcher et al., *Contraceptive Technology*, 17th ed. (New York: Irvington, 1998), 377.

6. A survey of 522 women revealed that about 90 percent of users report ease of use, ease of purchasing, and comfort as important advantages of vaginal barriers. In addition, users of the sponge reported satisfaction with twenty-four-hour protection regardless of number of acts of intercourse. This survey was sponsored by Allendale Pharmaceuticals, Inc., the makers of the Today Sponge, http://www.todaysponge.com/.

7. Stewart, "Vaginal Barriers," 384.

8. Costs and purchasing information for these products are from http://www.birthcontrol.com/.

Chapter 12 *Combined Hormonal Contraceptives*

1. The pill impacts liver function, clotting factors, blood viscosity, body water, hormones including insulin, growth hormone, adrenal steroids, thyroid hormones, prolactin, luteinizing hormone, follicle stimulating hormone, estrogen, and progesterone, and changes the minerals and vitamins present in the bloodstream including copper, zinc, vitamin A, K, B6, B12, C, riboflavin and folic acid, and factors that affect blood pressure, immunity, and allergy. John Guillebaud, *Contraception: Your Questions Answered* (London: Churchill Livingstone, 1999), 156.

2. The pill contains both estrogen and progestin (synthetic progesterone), which affect the body in different ways. Estrogen prevents ovulation by suppressing two key hormones that develop the egg, luteinizing hormone and follicle-stimulating hormone. Sometimes people say that the pill "tricks your body into thinking it's already pregnant," which refers to this hormonal suppression. Estrogen also alters the development of the endometrium, making it less receptive to implantation of a fertilized egg. Progestins prevent ovulation, thicken cervical fluid to hamper sperm movement, and make the endometrium less receptive to implantation of a fertilized egg.

3. Ian Thorneycroft and Sophia Cariati, "Ultra-Low-Dose Oral Contraceptives: Are They Right for Your Patient?" *Medscape Women's Health eJournal* 6 (2001).

4. Rarely, a woman may ovulate when using combined oral contraceptives because her natural hormones "override" the synthetic hormones. When ovulation occurs, it is more often due to a woman forgetting to take several pills at the beginning of her cycle, allowing her natural hormones to cause ovulation.

5. Seasonale contains the same hormones as other combined oral contraceptives but is taken with a new schedule. The pill is taken for eighty-four days, and then no pills are taken for seven days. A woman bleeds during this week, which comes only three to four times per year. In March 2002 clinical trials were being completed for Seasonale, and FDA approval was pending. "Pill to Cut Number of Periods," *BBC News*, 14 March 2002.

6. Information may be found at http://www.Lunelle.com.

7. Information may be found at http://www.orthomcneil.com. "FDA Updates," *FDA Consumer Magazine*, January–February 2002; and "FDA Approves First Hormonal Contraceptive Skin Patch," FDA Talk Paper T01-58, 20 November 2001.

8. Ortho-McNeil News Center, "First Birth Control Patch, Ortho Evra, Now Available by Prescription," 30 March 2002, http://www.orthomcneil.com/frames/news.htm. More information about the patch may be found at http://www.orthomcneil.com.

9. Information may be found at http://www.organon.com and http://www.nuvaring.com.

10. "Contraceptive Ring 'As Good As Pill,'" *BBC News*, 14 March 2001; "FDA Approves Vaginal Contraceptive Ring," 9 November 2001, http://www.newsnet5.com/.

11. Robert A. Hatcher and John Guillebaud, "The Pill: Combined Oral Contraceptives," in Robert Hatcher et al., *Contraceptive Technology*, 17th ed. (New York: Irvington, 1998), 408.

12. Barry Dickinson, "Drug Interactions Between Oral Contraceptives and Antibiotics," *Obstetrics and Gynecology* 98 (2001): 853–60.

13. George W. Creasy, "Contraceptive Efficacy and Cycle Control with the Ortho Evra/Evra Transdermal System: The Analysis of Pooled Data," *Fertility and Sterility* 77 (2002): S13–S18.

14. "FDA Approves First Hormonal Vaginal Contraceptive Ring," FDA Talk Paper T01-46, 3 October 2001.

15. A study of 5,317 women in Brazil showed that half of pill users had risk factors for complications yet were unaware of potential problems. C. Petta et al., "Users' Awareness of Factors Associated with Complications During Pill Use," *Advances in Contraception* 10 (1994): 257–64. Also, see Barry Dickinson, "Drug Interactions."

16. L. Potter, "'Pill' Failure and the Importance of Correct Use," *Fertility Control Reviews* 1 (1992): 3–10. Also see Paul Little et al., "Effect of Educational Leaflets and Questions on Knowledge of Contraception in Women Taking the Combined Contraceptive Pill: Randomized Controlled Trial," *British Medical Journal* 316 (1998): 1948–52.

17. Experts expect that the hormone-related advantages and disadvantages of injections, patch, and vaginal ring will be similar to the advantages and disadvantages associated with the birth control pill. Penelope Morrison Bosarge, "Update: Women and Contraception" (4th Annual Conference of the National Association of Nurse Practitioners in Women's Health, 2000).

18. M. H. Rahimy and K. K. Ryan, "Lunelle Monthly Contraceptive Injection: Assessment of Return of Ovulation after Three-Month Injections in Surgically Sterile Women," *Contraception* 60 (1999): 189–200.

19. Guillebaud, *Contraception: Your Questions Answered*, 101.

20. Ian Thorneycroft, "Cycle Control with Oral Contraceptives: A Review of the Literature," *American Journal of Obstetrics and Gynecology* 180 (1999): S280–S287.

21. Marcelle Cedars, "Triphasic Oral Contraceptives: Review and Comparison of Various Regimes," *Fertility and Sterility* 77 (2002): 1–14; Daniel Mishell, "Noncontraceptive Health Benefits of Oral Contraceptives," *Journal of Reproductive Medicine* 38 (1993): 1021–29; H. B. Peterson and N. C. Lee, "The Health Effects of Oral Contraceptives: Misperceptions, Controversies and Continuing Good News," *Clinical Obstetrics and Gynecology* 32, no. 2 (1989): 339–55; Thorneycroft, "Cycle Control." Possible benefits still being researched include a reduced risk for thyroid disease, rheumatoid arthritis, duodenal ulcers, and endometriosis. Guillebaud, *Contraception: Your Questions Answered*, 131. Also see National Cancer Institute Information Resources, "Oral Contraceptives and Cancer Risk," *Cancer Facts*, 2000. Hatcher and Guillebaud, "The Pill," 410.

22. Gail Walker, "Family History of Cancer, Oral Contraceptive User, and Ovarian Cancer Risk," *American Journal of Obstetrics and Gynecology* 186 (2002): 8–14.

23. Diane Thiboutot, "Ultra-Low-Dose Oral Contraceptive Effectively Treats Acne," *Fertil Steril* 76 (2001): 461–68.

24. One hundred British women who suffered severe cardiovascular complications they believe were associated with pill use sued several pharmaceutical companies. They claim they were not informed of risks when they began using the birth control pill. "A Bitter Pill," *The Guardian*, 27 February 2002; David Firn and Nikki Tait, "Third Generation Pill-Makers in Blood Clot Case," *Financial Times*, 4 March 2002; "Pill Caused Long-Term Damage," *BBC News*, 4 March 2002.

25. Anne Burke, "Report on the 2001 Annual Meeting of the Association of Reproductive Health Professionals," *Medscape Women's Health* 7 (2002); Guillebaud, *Contraception: Your Questions Answered*, 234; M. Rosenberg and M. S. Waugh, "Causes and Consequences of Oral Contraceptive Noncompliance," *American Journal of Obstetrics and Gynecology* 180 (1999): 276–79.

26. L. Moore, R. Valluck, C. McDougall, et al., "A Comparative Study of 1-Year Weight Gain Among Users of Medroxyprogesterone Acetate, Levonorgestrel Implants and Oral Contraceptives," *Contraception* 52 (1995):

215–20; Michael Rosenberg, "Weight Change with Oral Contraceptive Use and During the Menstrual Cycle: Results of Daily Measurements," *Contraception* 58 (1998): 345–49.

27. Elstein and H. Furniss, "The Fiction of an Ideal Hormonal Contraceptive," *Advances in Contraception* 12 (1996): 129–38; Peter Kovacs and Ursula Snyder, "57th Annual Meeting of the American Society for Reproductive Medicine," *Medscape Women's Health* (2001); M. J. Rosenberg, M. S. Burnhill, M. S. Waugh, et al., "Compliance and Oral Contraceptives: A Review," *Contraception* 52 (1995): 137–41.

28. S. Wysocki, "A Survey of Women and Healthcare Providers' Perceptions Regarding Oral Contraceptives and Weight Gain" (research presentation at 4th Annual Conference of the National Association of Nurse Practitioners in Women's Health, Orlando, October 2001).

29. W. Miller, "Why Some Women Fail to Use Their Contraceptive Method: A Psychological Investigation," *Family Planning Perspectives* 18 (1986): 27–32.

30. The two- to three-month delay may also be affected by physicians' advice to wait several cycles after stopping pill use before attempting to conceive. Guillebaud, *Contraception: Your Questions Answered*, 134.

31. Unless otherwise cited, information about major medical complications is from Helen C. Pymar and Mitchell Creinin, "The Risks of Oral Contraceptive Pills," *Seminars in Reproductive Medicine* 19 (2001): 305–12. Lunelle information is from "Patient Information about LUNELLE Monthly Contraceptive Injection," FDA labeling, 2001.

32. Diana Petitti et al., "Stroke in Users of Low-Dose Oral Contraceptives," *New England Journal of Medicine* 335 (1996): 8–15; Stephen Schwartz et al., "Stroke and Use of Low-Dose Oral Contraceptives in Young Women: A Pooled Analysis of Two US Studies," *Stroke* 29 (1998): 2277–84; WHO Collaborative Study, "Ischaemic Stroke and Combined Oral Contraceptives," *Lancet* 348 (1996): 498–505.

33. Ale Algra, "Third Generation Oral Contraceptives and Risk of Venous Thrombosis: Meta-Analysis," BMJ 323 (2001): 131–34; O. Lidegaard, B. Edstrom, and S. Kreiner, "Oral Contraceptives and Venous Thromboembolism: A Five-Year National Case-Control Study," *Contraception* 65, no. 3 (2002): 187–96; Jan Vandenbroucke, "Higher Risk of Venous Thrombosis During Early Use of Oral Contraceptives in Women with Inherited Clotting Defects," *Archives of Internal Medicine* 160 (2000): 49–52.

34. Guillebaud, *Contraception: Your Questions Answered*, 153.

35. Estrostep Patient Brief Summary, Pfizer Pharmaceuticals, 2001.

36. W. A. A. Van Os, D. Edelman, P. Rhemrev, and S. Grant, "Oral Contraceptives and Breast Cancer Risk," *Advances in Contraception* 13 (1997): 63–69.

37. "Patient Information about LUNELLE Monthly Contraceptive Injection," FDA labeling, 2001.

38. "FDA Updates," *FDA Consumer Magazine* (January–February 2002); Ortho-McNeil News Center, "The R.W. Johnson Pharmaceutical Research Institute Submits Application for FDA Approval of New Contraceptive ORTHO EVRA Transdermal System," 27 December 2000, http://www.ortho mcneil.com/frames/news.htm; "Contraceptive Patch Set for Europe," *BBC News*, 26 February 2002; "Contraceptive Patch Gets Thumbs Up," *BBC News*, 8 May 2001.

39. "Ortho Evra Fact Sheet," http://www.orthoevra.com/newsroom/pdfs/fact_sheet.pdf.

40. Hatcher and Guillebaud, "The Pill," 457.

41. Ibid., 409.

42. John F. Kippley and Sheila K. Kippley, *The Art of Natural Family Planning*, 4th ed. (Cincinnati: Couple to Couple League, 1999), 9; Chris Kahlenborn, essay submitted to U.S. FDA, 25 May 2000.

43. American Life League, http://www.all.org.

44. Susan A. Crockett, Joseph L. DeCook, Donna Harrison, and Camilla Hersh, "Using Hormone Contraceptives Is a Decision Involving Science, Scripture, and Conscience," in Kilner et al., eds., *The Reproduction Revolution*, 192–204.

Chapter 13 *Progestin-Only Contraceptives*

1. A progestin-only vaginal ring has been tested but is not yet FDA-approved. WHO Task Force on Long-Acting Systemic Agents for Fertility Regulation, "Microdose Intravaginal Levonorgestrel Contraception: A Multi-Centre Clinical Trial," *Contraception* 41 (1990): 105–24.

2. Pharmacia & Upjohn, *Depo-Provera Contraceptive Injection: Patient Information Guide* (pamphlet, New Jersey, 1999).

3. "Choices: Progestin-Only Pills or 'Mini-Pills,'" http://www.managing contraception.com/choices/ch-pop.html.

4. There are two types of hormones available as injections. Depo-Provera contains depot-medroxyprogesterone acetate (DMPA) and Noristerat contains norethindrone enanthate (NET-EN).

5. Horacio Croxatt, "Progestin Implants for Female Contraception," *Contraception* 65, no. 1 (2002): 15–19; Olav Meirik, "Implantable Contraceptives for Women," *Contraception* 65, no. 1 (2002): 1–2.

6. Implants have been used globally for many years and were introduced to the United States in 1990. Initially, Norplant was popular in the United States but use declined by 90 percent by 1996 due to a lawsuit and media attention surrounding difficult removals. The use of implants has increased since that time, but implants remain less popular than the birth control pill. Polly Harrison and Allan Rosenfield, "Research, Introduction, and Use: Advancing from Norplant," *Contraception* 58, no. 6 (1998): 323–34.

7. Robert A. Hatcher, "Depo-Provera, Norplant, and Progestin-Only Pills (Minipills)," in Robert Hatcher et al., *Contraceptive Technology*, 17th ed. (New York: Irvington, 1998), 470.

8. M. F. McCann and L. S. Potter, "Progestin-Only Oral Contraception: A Comprehensive Review," *Contraception* 50 (1994 Supplement): S1–195.

9. Anna Glasier, "Implantable Contraceptives for Women: Effectiveness, Discontinuation Rates, Return of Fertility, and Outcome of Pregnancies," *Contraception* 65, no. 1 (2002): 29–37.

10. Bleeding stops for around 40 percent of Depo-Provera users, 20 to 30 percent of users of progestin-releasing IUDs, and most minipill users. "Progestin-Only Contraceptives," *Pocket Guide for Family Planning Service Providers*, Reproductive Health Online, Johns Hopkins University, 2000, http://www.reproline.jhu.edu/english/6read/6multi/pg/index.htm.

11. "Progestin-only Injectables FAQ," http://www.fhi.org/en/fp/fpfaq/fpfaqs/fpfaq5a.html.

12. Most research on side effects of injections has been on Depo-Provera. See Pharmacia and Upjohn, *Depo-Provera Contraceptive Injection Patient Guide* (Kalamazoo, Mich.), 9, and Gale Research Group, *Gale Encyclopedia of Medicine* (1999), s.v. "Depo-Provera," http://www.gale.com. Though depression is considered a side effect of both Depo-Provera and Norplant, two recent studies have found no association between these methods and depression. Carolyn Westerhoff et al., "Depressive Symptoms and Depo-Provera," *Contraception* 57 (1998): 237–40; Carolyn Westerhoff et. al., "Depressive Symptoms and Norplant Contraceptive Implants," *Contraception* 57 (1998): 241–45.

13. Robert A. Hatcher, "Depo-Provera, Norplant, and Progestin-Only Pills (Minipills)," in Hatcher et al., *Contraceptive Technology*, 476.

14. Pharmacia and Upjohn, *Depo-Provera Patient Guide*, 16; K. Singh and G. C. Chye, "Adverse Effects Associated with Contraceptive Implants: Incidence, Prevention and Management," *Advances in Contraception* 14 (1998): 1–13.

15. Pharmacia and Upjohn, *Depo-Provera Patient Guide*, 13.

16. Tim Cundy et al., "Spinal Bone Density in Women Using Depot Medroxyprogesterone Contraception," *Obstetrics and Gynecology* 92 (1998): 569–73.

17. Robert A. Hatcher, "Depo-Provera, Norplant, and Progestin-Only Pills (Minipills)," in Hatcher et al., *Contraceptive Technology*, 501; *Gale Encyclopedia of Medicine*, s.v. "Depo-Provera."

18. Most research on implants has been on the Norplant system. Within five years of beginning Norplant use, 50 percent of women request removal due to unacceptable side effects. Ian S. Fraser et al., "Norplant Consensus Statement and Background Review," *Contraception* 57 (1998): 1–9. For additional information on unpleasant side effects of progestin-only contraceptives, see Nuriye Ortayli, "Users' Perspectives on Implantable Contraceptives for Women," *Contraception* 65, no. 1 (2002): 107–11; Robert A. Hatcher, "Depo-

Provera, Norplant, and Progestin-Only Pills (Minipills)," in Hatcher et al., *Contraceptive Technology*, 494.

19. Irving Sivin et al., "Levonorgestrel Capsule Implants in the United States: A 5-Year Study," *Obstetrics and Gynecology* 92 (1998): 337–44.

20. S. Klavon and G. Grubb, "Insertion Site Complications During the First Year of Norplant Use," *Contraception* 41 (1990): 27–37.

21. "Choices: Norplant Implants," http://www.managingcontraception.com/choices/ch-norplant.html.

22. Robert A. Hatcher, "Depo-Provera, Norplant, and Progestin-Only Pills (Minipills)," in Hatcher et al., *Contraceptive Technology*, 503.

23. Ibid., 472.

Chapter 14 *Emergency Contraception*

1. M. Swahn et al., "Effect of Post-coital Contraceptive Methods on the Endometrium and the Menstrual Cycle," Acta Obstetricia et Gynecologica Scandinavia 75 (1996): 738–44.

2. L. Marions et al., "Emergency Contraception with Mifepristone and Levonorgestrel: Mechanism of Action," Obstetrics and Gynecology 100, no. 1 (2002): 65–71.

3. Research on these effects is ongoing, and no clear scholarly consensus has yet emerged. A. Glasier, "Emergency Postcoital Contraception," *New England Journal of Medicine* 337 (1997): 1058–64; M. Swahn, "Effect of Post-Coital Contraceptive Methods."

4. ECPs currently used in the United States include high-dose estrogen pills, the Yuzpe regimen, which includes estrogen and progestin, progestin-only dosages, and Danazol.

5. M. Sanders Wanner and R. Couchenour, "Hormonal Emergency Contraception," *Pharmacotherapy* 22, no. 1 (2002): 43–53.

6. Hatcher et al., *A Pocket Guide to Managing Contraception*, 1999–2000 ed. (Tiger, Ga.: Bridging the Gap Communications), 69.

7. Task Force on Postovulatory methods of Fertility Regulation, "Randomized Controlled Trial of Levonorgestrel Versus the Yuzpe Regimen of Combined Oral Contraceptives for Emergency Contraception," *Lancet* 352 (1998): 428–33.

8. Charlotte Ellertson et al., "Emergency Contraception," *Seminars in Reproductive Medicine* 19, no. 4 (2001): 323–30.

9. James Trussell and Charlotte Ellertson, "Efficacy of Emergency Contraception," *Fertility Control Review* 4 (1995): 8–11.

10. Unless otherwise noted, information about advantages and disadvantages of emergency contraceptives is from Paul F. A. Van Look and Felicia Stewart, "Emergency Contraception," in Robert Hatcher et al., *Contraceptive Technology*, 17th ed. (New York: Irvington, 1998), 277–302.

11. Robert A. Hatcher et al., *A Personal Guide to Managing Contraception for Women and Men* (Tiger, Ga.: Bridging the Gap Communications, 2000), 71.

12. Plan B Patient Information Guide (Women's Capitol Corporation, n.d.); Preven Patient Information Guide (Gynetics Inc., 1998).

13. Robert Hatcher et al., *A Pocket Guide*, 63.

Chapter 15 *Intrauterine Devices*

1. John Guillebaud, *Contraception: Your Questions Answered* (London: Churchill Livingstone, 1999), 339–426. Gary K. Stewart, "Intrauterine Devices (IUDs)," in Robert Hatcher et al., *Contraceptive Technology*, 17th ed. (New York: Irvington, 1998), 511–44. Articles detailing the shift in medical opinion about the IUD include K. L. Dardano and R. T. Burkman, "The Intrauterine Contraceptive Device: An Often-Forgotten and Maligned Method of Contraception," *American Journal of Obstetrics and Gynecology* 181 (July 1999): 1–5; Daniel R. Mishell Jr., "Intrauterine Devices: Mechanisms of Action, Safety, and Efficacy," *Contraception* 58 (1998): 45S–53S; W. A. A. Van Os, "The Intrauterine Device and Its Dynamics," *Advances in Contraception* 15 (1999): 119–32.

2. Paragard T 380A Intrauterine Copper Contraceptive Prescribing Information Leaflet (Raritan, N.J.: Ortho-McNeil, 2002).

3. Progestasert Intrauterine Progesterone Contraceptive System Prescribing Information Leaflet (Palo Alto, Calif.: ALZA Corporation, 1996).

4. Gary K. Stewart, "Intrauterine Devices (IUDs)," in Hatcher et al., *Contraceptive Technology*, 513.

5. A. E. Lethaby, I. Cooke, and M. Rees, "Progesterone/progestogen Releasing Intrauterine Systems versus Either Placebo or Any Other Medication for Heavy Menstrual Bleeding (Cochrane Review)," in *The Cochrane Library* (Oxford: Update Software, 2000), 2.

6. Olav Istre and Birgitta Trolle, "Levonorgestrel IUD Comparable to Endometrial Resection for Menorrhagia," *Fertility and Sterility* 76 (2001): 304–9.

7. A. G. Khomassuridze et al., "Intrauterine Device and Pelvic Inflammatory Disease," *Advances in Contraception* 13 (1997): 71–78.

8. UN Development Programme et al., "Long Term Reversible Contraception: Twelve Years of Experience with the Tcu380A and Tcu220C," *Contraception* 56 (1997): 341–52.

9. Gary K. Stewart, "Intrauterine Devices (IUDs)," in Hatcher et al., *Contraceptive Technology*, 516.

10. Ibid., 520. A recent literature review concludes that loss of menstruation is the primary reason for discontinuing the levonorgestrel IUD. R. French et al., "Hormonally Impregnated Intrauterine Systems (IUSs), versus Other Forms of Reversible Contraceptives as Effective Methods of Preventing Preg-

nancy (Cochrane Review)," in *The Cochrane Library* (Oxford: Update Software, 2001), 2.

11. John Stanbak and David Grimes, "Can Intrauterine Device Removals for Bleeding or Pain be Predicted at a One-Month Follow-Up Visit? A Multivariate Analysis," *Contraception* 58 (1999): 357–60.

12. Gary K. Stewart, "Intrauterine Devices (IUDs)," in Hatcher et al., *Contraceptive Technology*, 516.

13. Ibid., 536.

14. I. Sivin, J. Stern, E. Coutinho, et al., "Prolonged Intrauterine Contraception: A Seven-Year Randomized Study of the Levonorgestrel 20 mcg/ay (LNg20) and the Copper T380 Ag IUDs," *Contraception* 44 (1991): 473–80; J. Toivonen, T. Luukkainen, and H. Allonen, "Protective Effect of Intrauterine Release of Levonorgestrel on Pelvic Infection: Three Years' Comparative Experience of Levonorgestrel- and Copper-Releasing Intrauterine Devices," *Obstetrics and Gynecology* 77 (1991): 261–64.

15. Gary K. Stewart, "Intrauterine Devices (IUDs)," in Hatcher et al., *Contraceptive Technology*, 540.

16. Ibid., 514.

Chapter 16 *Male and Female Sterilization*

1. C. M. Marquette et al., "Vasectomy in the United States, 1991," *American Journal of Public Health* 85 (1995): 644–49.

2. Planned Parenthood Federation of America, "All about Vasectomy," *Journal of the American Medical Association Contraception Information Center*, 1995, http://www.ama-assn.org.

3. Gary K. Stewart and Charles S. Carignan, "Female and Male Sterilization," in Robert Hatcher et al., *Contraceptive Technology*, 17th ed. (New York: Irvington, 1998), 546. A recent study reports that pregnancies after vasectomy may be underreported in the United States. A study of Nepalese men showed seventeen out of one thousand couples became pregnant within one year of vasectomy. This higher rate may, in fact, be due to underreporting in other studies, or it may be due to the vasectomy procedures or patient follow-through used in Nepal. "Pregnancies More Common Than Expected after Vasectomy," *Family Health International News Release*, 10 September 2001.

4. Stewart and Carignan, "Female and Male Sterilization," 569.

5. Knowles and Ringel, *All About Birth Control*, 176.

6. Ibid., 184.

7. B. Healy, "From the National Institutes of Health: Does Vasectomy Cause Prostate Cancer?" *Journal of the American Medical Association* 269 (1993): 2620. Controversy over vasectomies and prostate cancer in the early 1990s did not affect vasectomy acceptance or practice in the United States. R. J. Magnani et al., "Vasectomy in the United States, 1991 and 1995," *American Journal of Public Health* 89 (1999): 92–94.

8. Stewart and Carignan, "Female and Male Sterilization," 553.

9. Planned Parenthood Federation of America, "All about Tubal Sterilization," *Journal of the American Medical Association Contraception Information Center*, http://www.ama-assn.org (1998).

10. Barbara Barnett, "Search for Nonsurgical Sterilization Continues," *Network* 18, no. 1 (1997), http://www.fhi.org/en/fp/fppubs/network/v18%2D1nt1815.html; Lauran Neergaard, "Nonsurgical sterilization for women approved," *Columbia (S.C.) State*, 5 November 2002, A3.

11. Stewart and Carignan, "Female and Male Sterilization," 546.

12. Ibid., 572.

13. World Health Organization, "Mental Health and Female Sterilization: Report of a WHO Collaborative Prospective Study," *Journal of Biosocial Science* 16 (1984): 1–21.

14. Herbert B. Peterson et al., "The Risk of Ectopic Pregnancy after Tubal Sterilization," *New England Journal of Medicine* 336 (13 March 1997): 762–67.

15. Herbert B. Peterson et al., "The Risk of Menstrual Abnormalities after Tubal Sterilization," *The New England Journal of Medicine* 343 (7 December 2000): 1681–87. Family Health International studied menstrual pattern changes in 1,550 women at 45 hospitals in 23 countries. Slightly more than half reported no change in their menstrual patterns a year after sterilization, and 47 percent reported changes. The changes included both improvements and changes for the worse. Women with abnormal menstrual cycles were more likely to experience abnormalities after sterilization than women with normal cycles. Women who quit the pill or IUD were more likely to report menstrual changes. These changes are probably due to the stoppage of the pill or IUD and not to sterilization. Family Health International, "Does Female Sterilization Affect Menstrual Patterns?" *Family Health International Frequently Asked Questions*, www.fhi.org, 1999.

16. L. G. Escobedo et al., "Case-Fatality Rates for Tubal Sterilization in U.S. Hospitals, 1979 to 1980," *American Journal of Obstetrics and Gynecology* 160 (1989): 147–50.

17. Sarah Keller, "Female Sterilization Safe, Very Effective," *Network* 18, no. 1 (1997), http://www.fhi.org/en/fp/fppubs/network/v18%2D1/nt1812.html.

18. Stewart and Carignan, "Female and Male Sterilization," 548.

19. Ibid.

Jenell Williams Paris (Ph.D., American University) is an associate professor of anthropology at Bethel College in St. Paul, Minnesota. She is a fertility awareness instructor with Fertility Awareness–Twin Cities.